CHANGES FOR THE BETTER

Reprinted from 'Old & Young in Elizabeth's Days'
and other articles

by

G. M. ALEXANDER

with slight additions

Volume 2

Published by Zoar Publications, 44 Queens Drive, Ossett,
W. Yorks. England WF5 OND.

1978

ZOAR PUBLICATIONS
44 Queens Drive, Ossett, W. Yorks WF5 0ND

ISBN 0 904435 19 9

Printed in Great Britain by
O. & M. Ltd., 1 Rugby Street, Leicester LE3 5FF

ACKNOWLEDGEMENTS

In sending forth this further volume, I acknowledge the kind and ready help that has been given me, and permission to reproduce from a variety of sources as follows:

To the family of the late Miss G. M. Alexander for permission to reproduce and edit the first sixteen chapters, which originally appeared in her book '*Old and Young in Elizabeth's Days*' (Farncombe & Co. Ltd.) and as 'Puritan Stories' in the *Little Gleaner*:

To Timothy Abbott, ARIBA, for the meticulous time-charts and maps throughout the book, and the dustjacket:

To K. W. H. Howard for much help in supplying and checking information, and the use of some illustrations:

To Cheshire County Record Office for the use of illustrations from their extra-illustrated copy of Ormerod's *History of Cheshire* (1818 edn) on pages 2, 6, 18, 20, 21, 23, 24, 25, 29, 31, 44, 83 and 95:

To Pauline Smith for the drawings on pages 5 and 76:

To Suffolk Records Office for their kind permission to use illustrations on pages 36, 37 and 39; and through them to the rector of Bramford, Rev. G. Christian for permission to reproduce the signature on page 36:

To the Bodleian Library for the signature of Dod from the Rawlinson MSS reproduced on page 48, and for the signatures of Harris and Whateley consulted and quoted by permission of the Keeper of the Archives, Oxford University, and reproduced on pages 60 and 64:

To G. G. Walker, Esq., of Bodicote, Banbury, for the drawing on page 70:

To Hertfordshire County Records Office for the illustrations on pages 77 and 132, and Herbert Palmer's signature on page 130:

To Derbyshire County Library: Derby Local Studies Department for the use of the illustrations in Rawlins' *Churches and Chapels in the County of Derby* reproduced on pages 82, 85 and 103:

To Preston parish records deposited at the Lancashire Record Office [PR 2845], for the drawing on page 101.

To the British Library Board for their kind permission to reproduce Add. MS. 32467 on pages 92 and 93.

Mr. W. G. Walker, *The History of Oundle Schools* (The Grocers' Company) has also been of absorbing interest and usefulness.

D. Oldham

Stamford, 1978.

CONTENTS

Bruen-Stapleford

THE Squire of Bruen-Stapleford (some six miles east of Chester) was considered by Perkins the Cambridge divine to be the foremost man in England for promoting the cause of God in his own county. His name, like his father's, was John Bruen; his old family crest was a fisherman with a staff in his right hand, holding a landing-net over his shoulder with his left hand. John Bruen of this era followed Christ and He made him a fisher of men. He was once asked when the Lord began the work of grace in his soul. He answered, he did not know; but he remembered that when he was six years old in 1566, his father was angry with him one day; and he, going to pray in his father's private chapel, "found comfort and inexpressible joy"; and the next day he went to the same place and used the same means, but found that he could not get the same comfort.

At the age of fourteen he was sent to a school in Dutton for three years but learned little. The school was conducted on the same lines as it had always been; the boys had little academic and no religious teaching; they heard a sermon once a year, and all the Sundays were given up to sport. But at Oxford John learned why certain old Popish superstitions to which he had always been used in the country were wrong. His heart was opened to receive instruction from books and from the conversation of a Chester friend, John Brerewood, who drew his attention to 1 Timothy 4, and from that passage he believed Popery to be a seducing spirit in "forbidding to marry and commanding to abstain from meats."

After his return from Oxford his father advised him to marry Miss Elizabeth Hardware of Bromborough Hall, in

ARMS OF BRUEN OF BRUEN STAPLEFORD

Wirral, whom he considered a pious girl. John was deferential and obedient; he liked her and they were married in 1580 when he was 20. When in 1587, he had three

1550   1600   1630

M   Elizabeth I   James I

Married Elizabeth Hardware

JOHN BRUEN 1560-1625

children, his father died and he was left the head of the house and owner of Bruen-Stapleford. For some time past all his pleasures had seemed empty; hunting and falconry had left him dissatisfied, and now at his father's death, he longed to know that if *he* should die it would be well with his soul. His wife had similar longings. They 'had great conflicts with carnal reason,' and 'both were much given to prayer,' as William Hinde his biographer writes; 'and when they began to taste the pleasures of religion they soon gave up the pleasures of sin which are but for a season, and both happily succeeded in bringing others to seek the Lord. They were *changes for the better.*

These 'others' were his brothers and sisters and his mother.

John, as the eldest of the large family, had twelve portions to provide for his brothers and sisters. So he was obliged to cut down expenses; a deer-park had to be thrown open; falconry, being a very expensive pastime, he dropped, and instead, increased his fishponds, dove-cotes, and rabbit-warrens. Besides the large farm he owned two mills in Chester, and the blessing of God increased everything until, as he said, he discharged "every punctilio, blessed be God," of his father's will.

It would seem that his mother with seven of her younger children still remained at the Hall. They were always present at the family worship he set up, and his grown-up brothers often came; it was blessed to the conversion of some of them and of some of the servants. Sometimes these family prayers, with singing, prayer, reading and the squire's exposition of a chapter of the Bible, made quite a service.

Robert Passfield, one of the servants, a faithful old

JOHN BRUEN OF BRUEN-STAPLEFORD

retainer who could not read, had an excellent gift in prayer, and his master often asked him to pray. His master often asked him too to repeat the sermons he had heard for the benefit of those that couldn't get. Old Robert gave this a great deal of thought – he could not write but he did want to remember. So he had a brainwave: he got a wide leather belt or girdle long enough to go twice round his waist: he marked on it divisions, one for each book of the Bible; for chapters, Robert fixed points or thongs of leather, making points by fives and tens to distinguish the chapters of that book; and by other points he divided the chapters into contents or verses as needed. Now he was ready! Coming home after a service, he found he could repeat the sermons, quoting the texts referred to without any bother at all! I guess the children of John Bruen and his wife Elizabeth, eight of them (John, James, Henry, Calvin, Beza, Nathaniel, Anne and Elizabeth!) watched old Robert using his girdle with wide-open eyes! After old Robert had passed away, Mr

THE OPEN BIBLE IN THE HALL

Bruen hung up the leather girdle in his study, smilingly calling it 'the girdle of verity.'

It was not long before this kind of life brought hatred and ridicule. His house was the only one the gentry knew where such Puritanism held sway—a large Bible placed open on a desk in the hall, and another, open on a desk in the great parlour! Convocation in Grindal's time had ordered this; the

QUEEN ELIZABETH I

order should have been observed in all the baronial halls. But by this time not many except the Puritan gentry evidenced that love of the Scriptures which marked "the beginning of days."

Having proprietary rights in the church of Tarvin Mr. Bruen cleared it of images and of stained glass windows, which depicted the holy Trinity. He said the stained glass darkened the light of the church and obscured the light of the Gospel: so he had it all removed and replaced with clear glass. That too was only according to the Queen's own rule, "utterly to extinguish and destroy all manner of idolatry." But the people did not like it. The incumbent was a careless, lazy priest, one of the abounding 'Vicars of Bray,' to whom all religions were alike, and Mr. Bruen was alone in his wish for practical reformation. "I was like a pelican in the wilderness in those days," he said, "and like an owl in the desert. My enemies reproached me all the day, and were moved against me." But happiness was before him—the gospel-tide was rising. He would ride thirty or forty miles to find proper preachers, and he found several in Lancashire: Mr. Harrison of Childwall, "one of the Preachers appointed by her Majestie for the Countie Palatine of Lancaster"; William Leigh, Pastor of Standish; Mr. Pendlebury, Mr. Arthur Storrer, and Mr. Sabbath Clark. In time he arranged that a Reformation 'lecture' was preached every month at Tarvin Church.

The old incumbent gladly suffered these better preachers to occupy his unloved place in the pulpit. But they were mocked and slighted by the people. Mr. Bruen then withdrew Mr. Storrer from the church and appointed him chaplain in the Hall. Here great blessing attended his preaching to the tenants, so that presently Tarvin too welcomed the preachers. After the days of Queen Elizabeth, all through the Civil War, when Sabbath Clark was the Rector, it was like a city set on a hill, and was not hid: he had become curate at Tarvin in 1611, the year the Authorised Version was brought out, until he was instituted vicar there in 1622: there he continued to labour, after Mr. Bruen's death in 1625, right through to 1662 till his ejection under the

Act of Uniformity; six or seven months later this honoured servant of the Lord passed to his heavenly rest.

The Romish holy days—May Day, Whitsuntide and Midsummer (St. John's Day) had long been occasions of sport and revelry—cruel sport, such as bull and bear-baiting, and immoral revels. On Midsummer night fires were lit in the fields, sometimes wood fires and sometimes bone fires, or bonfires. The people danced around them and jumped over them, screaming and tossing each other about with shouting and ribald songs. They were the St. John's fires, direct successors of the fires through which children had been passed to Moloch, as we read in the Bible (2 Kings 16. 3; 17. 17; 21. 6).

Setting his face against these customs, Bruen called preachers to Stapleford. Though at first all who attended the services were derided, a change came, and as so often in revival times, many who went to mock were quickened into divine life. On these occasions the Hall was an open house for guests; many came from long distances and the hospitality was on a great scale. They were welcome too to bring their children, and many a little Samuel had doubtless "whispered to his mother and said, 'Mother, this is a very good man's house, let us stay here a good while' " *(Pilgrim's Progress)*.

Between the services there was conversation, and great grace was upon them, so that the time was not frittered away, but fearing God they delighted to hear from one another what He had done for their souls. It was said that from these high days 'a plentiful harvest of souls grew up,' and that it was the chief means of the gospel being planted in other places in Cheshire after the Reformation.

Now whereas at first Mr. Bruen had no one like-minded amongst the Cheshire county families, it was his happy lot to gain the admiration and love of some of them. They wished to show their growing children what a home could be when conducted as he conducted his. He 'tabled' many such (i.e. they lived with him), just as old earls in earlier times 'tabled' their pages. Young Sir Richard Grosvenor and young Sir John Done were his guests, and the newly-married daughter-in-law of Chancellor Egerton went to learn there what it was to look well to the ways of a household. John Bruen once went into Sir John Done's room, which was unoccupied, and found a pack of cards on the mantelpiece, so he quietly removed the four 'knaves' and burnt them: he knew there were better things to spend their time on than those. He prayed for the conversion of such guests and in some instances his prayers were granted. He sometimes had over twenty of these 'boarders' at a time.

On one occasion he entertained his brother-in-law John Hardware, with his wife, children and servants, for many weeks. Mr. Hardware found at Bruen-Stapleford much more religion than he liked, and his host rebuked him for swearing. He found this intolerable and chafed under it. But one evening Mr. Bruen chose Psalm 141 for the portion, and several of his family one after another spoke on the words: "Let the righteous smite me, it shall be a kindness," he, like a moderator at a Prophesying, "summing all up." It might be thought that only a bow at a venture has the blessing of God. But as happened frequently in Mr. Bruen's house what was said was blessed; Mr. Hardware accepted it with meekness, and Mr. Bruen had far more than he asked or thought, in his case. In many, no reformation of life followed and he had to 'hope' for more, but both Mr. Hardware and his wife went home truly converted to God after that visit.

Mrs. Hardware secretly wondered what difference her husband would make in their manner of life in their own family, and with the tribe of servants. She had not long to wait; the first evening after their return he set up family worship, singing, reading, praying and *catechising*. She was overcome with gratitude, and never ceased to thank God for their visit to Bruen-Stapleford.

Some years after, in 1599, Mr. Hardware was elected Mayor of Chester, and it was he who 'would not consent to have the Devil for the butchers' at the Marching Watch in Midsummer, which I will tell you about another time.

Mr. Bruen lost his first dear wife Elizabeth, and after some while he married again: his second wife was Ann, the daughter of John Fox, and they had nine children – Abigail,

Jonathan, Obadiah, Joseph, Margaret and four more. I do not know how many of John Bruen's seventeen children lived to grow up to adult life, but I think they all loved their father greatly, and knew how he used the various rooms of their comfortable Stapleford Hall for his private worship, and the spots in the gardens, orchards, woods and fields where he delighted to commune with his best Friend.

Talking of what he did with the playing-cards reminds me of what a doctor said once in court. Years ago Dr. Gregory was witness in a case at the Scottish bar in Edinburgh. The doctor's testimony was to prove one of the parties insane. Being cross-examined, the doctor admitted that the person in question played admirably at whist.

"And do you seriously say, doctor," asked the learned counsel, "that a person having a capacity for a game so difficult, and which requires such memory, judgment and concentration, can be at the same time deranged in his understanding?"

"I am no card-player," said the doctor – solemnly, "but I have read in history that cards were invented for the amusement of an insane king, Charles VI of France." His reply decided the case.

But were the Puritans then against all recreation? Of course not; they did not like games of chance, but games like chess that developed skill and knowledge they felt were really recreations. You will see what Paul Bains said on page 41, and I will tell you later what Henry Scudder had to say about it too (see page 71).

Brettergholt

MR. BRUEN'S sister Catherine was nearly twenty years younger than he, and lived the first twenty years of her life at Bruen-Stapleford. She shared her brother's eagerness to hear good sermons and went miles, no doubt with him, to hear them. In the year 1599 she became the wife of William Brettergh of "Brettergholt nere Leverpole." And now, leaving her brother, let us follow Catherine.

MRS. CATHERINE BRETTERGH

After the marriage they would cross the river Mersey by a little ferry-boat to Hale, and ride or drive for a few miles to

Catherine Bruen became wife of William Brettergh

BRUEN STAPLEFORD

the ancient "holt" (i.e. shelter) to which new brides in the family had ridden for three centuries. The name Brettergholt is off the map now; the house was burnt down, but there remain to this day the stables and cowbyres. They stand round two sides of a very large square farmyard. The same garden too is there, and the same orchard, as if to illustrate in living green those annals of the young early Protestant wife, which describe Catherine Brettergh as sitting there reading, sometimes 'Foxe's *Book of Martyrs*' and sometimes chapters of the Bible.

The same two private roads cross the fields now as then. William used to be upset, when they were driving to church, if the coachman found the paths not exactly smooth, and it took Catherine's soothing words to dissuade him from surprise that they were rough. She wished he would not take arrears of rent from his cottage tenants; she felt they could not afford it, and made it up to them by kindnesses which endeared her to them.

William Brettergh was a very fervent Protestant and a magistrate. No one of his own standing in the neighbourhood upheld him. His near neighbours the Norrises of Speke Hall, were as yet giving all their influence to the cause of Popery; the Jesuits grew strong under their shadow. Soon after their marriage, William got up in the morning on two occasions to find that dastardly deeds had been done in the night; most of his horses and cattle had been maimed and their tails cut off.

His stock was chiefly in horses and cattle, and his fields were pasture land. Catherine could not but wish that the eyes of the people might be opened to the malicious deeds of which Popery was capable. For as far as the news travelled there was no doubt of this being the work of Papists. 'The case of the Brettergh cattle' is described in Court records as 'those great outrages of late committed by Catholics, not without the designments of pestilential seminaries that lurk amongst them.' The pestilential seminaries were schools of Jesuits. Jesuits were said to swarm like hornets in those parts. No one believed for a moment that any recusant Papist, fined perhaps for not going to church, would revenge himself by perpetrating cruelty on such a scale, without Jesuit instigation.

And so Brettergholt was not perhaps so snug a shelter to Catherine as her old home had been. "Jehovah nissi" appears upon the Brettergh crest; surely it was *this* William who adopted it; this period in any case was a green spot in the old family history.

Not for long did William have Catherine. In May 1601 she was attacked with ague. It may have been from the nearness of stretches of bog land; but whatever the cause she died after little more than a week's illness. At first she was very depressed, and her depression increased until she called herself a wretched, forsaken woman, condemned for being proud of her beauty. Delirium came, and she raved about the cattle; when that ceased, after brief intervals of calm, temptations came that she was forbidden to pray, was not one of the elect, and that she saw the Fire close beside her. These were bands in her death, but she was delivered from them and was comforted.

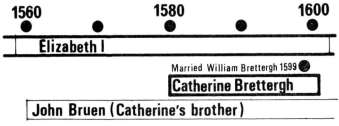

Friends came to see her from Toxteth. Her brother John Bruen came; and Mr. Harrison the Vicar of Childwall, her minister. What they said she received. But on the day before she died, her husband sat down at her bedside and read the seventeenth chapter of John's Gospel. While he read she was filled with great joy. For five hours she poured out praise and blessing, saying: "Oh, my sweet Saviour, shall I be with Thee? Oh, the joys! they are wonderful, wonderful, wonderful! Oh, it was a roaring wilderness, but this is sweeter than the Garden of Eden!" She died the last day of May on a Sabbath evening, saying with a sweet expression, "My warfare is accomplished. Lord, whom have I in heaven but Thee?" It was a *change for the better*, her last and best.

During her illness rumours spread in the neighbourhood that Mistress Brettergh was dying in despair; and in a very few days, that she *had* died in despair. To some these tidings were sad; many of them were quiet Papists to whom she had been kind and neighbourly; their religion was, as her relative William Fox said: "I believe as my father believed; God have mercy on his sweet soul." They were sorry to hear that she died in a religion proved wrong, as they thought, by the manner of her death. Others, zealous Papists, who looked upon the Jesuit seminaries as their tower of strength, were glad to hear and to spread that she had died in despair; it was a great triumph and they would go to the funeral to hear how the heretic ministers, whom they hated, bore the discomfiture.

Catherine's funeral took place on June 3rd 1601, the Wednesday after Whitsunday, one of the holidays, perhaps the last in the week, which had for so long been devoted at Bruen-Stapleford to the special sermons and to entertaining strangers. It was a wonderful providence that brought it to that day. Childwall church, where Mr. Brettergh had his family pew, was well attended. The hearse came, decked with long epitaphs of rugged poetry, but without crosses or pardon-letters in or on the coffin. But it was not because of the spectacle that Catherine's friends were grateful it fell on a holiday, but because of the sermons the people would hear—two very long sermons, one before the burial in the morning, and one in the afternoon.

The morning sermon was preached by Mr. Harrison; his text, Isaiah 57. 1: "The righteous perisheth." He spoke of the righteous as those to whom Christ's righteousness is imputed—a new doctrine there. "And it is strange," he said, "to see the partiality of Papists in the matter of imputation, for they teach that the fastings and satisfactory deeds of one, may be available to others, and yet deny that the righteousness of Christ may be imputed unto us for justification: as if the Lord would accept the works of men to satisfy for us, and not the righteousness of His own Son."

The sermon went on to work out, at length, what some of the real mourners amongst the Romanists wanted to hear, viz., the manner of death and what is proved by it. They had hitherto believed that if a man died like a lamb he was saved. In popish times it was regarded as a proof that his purgatory would soon give place to heaven, and who does not know how the "dying like a lamb" theory has lingered? Mr. Harrison told them that sudden death was not a judgment to the righteous, that ravings often came through disease, and that the devil, who cannot assault the saints in glory, often attacks them before they are there, while the wicked have no bands in their death. These views were new to many, and Mr. Harrison told the people where to find them in the Bible. Then he told them about the dying triumphs of Catherine Brettergh—that she said she was happy that ever she was born, to see that blessed day, and he said, "We should rather praise God for the victory than speak evil of her for the combat."

The funeral ended and the people dispersed, but to come again in the afternoon. Mr. Leigh of Standish said he had been asked "by the saddest saint in all the assembly" to preach; and added, "and I did not consult with flesh and blood, but have as you see most willingly obeyed the heavenly call." The purpose of the second sermon was comfort. Mr. Leigh took for his text, "Peace shall come," the old rendering of "They shall enter into peace" (Isaiah 57. 2).

In the course of his sermon, he went off into proofs against purgatory and praying to saints, probably new to the people. "The doctrine I aim at," he said, "is to prove that God never suffereth His elect to depart this life comfortless, nor will call them hence till they have seen, with Simeon, the Lord's Christ, either in spirit or body, or both." At some time in *this* life they are brought to Him. He then told them of his neighbour and friend, John Holland of Upholland and Heaton Hall, a minister who had just died. He had been sitting with him in his last illness the day before he died, when Mr. Holland had called for a Bible, saying, "Come, come; death approaches. Let us gather some flowers to comfort this hour." He turned to Romans 8 and asked him to read; after each verse, he asked Mr. Leigh to pause while Mr. Holland himself gave the meaning of his passage to comfort himself and the friends with him. Two hours went by in this way when Mr. Holland suddenly cried out, "O stop reading! What brightness is this I see? Have you lighted any candles?" "No," Mr. Leigh had said, "it is the sunshine," for it was about five o'clock on a clear summer's evening. "Sunshine," the dying man had said. "No, it is my Saviour's shine. Now farewell, world: welcome, heaven. The Daystar from on high has visited my heart. O speak when I am gone, and preach at my funeral, 'God dealeth familiarly with man'. Then the next morning, after speaking again so happily, like their young friend just departed, he said, "Amen, amen! Come, Lord Jesus, come quickly!" and fell asleep.

The sermon comforted the bereaved husband. He printed it, writing to Mr. Leigh: "I do it neither to your praise nor my own, but with a single eye to set out the Lord's glory. And for the wantonness of the world, the iniquity of the time, and the multitude of malicious wrestlers of whom you speak, let them alone while they but pine themselves in feeding upon our best things. Your assured in Christ Jesus, William Brettergh."

It was a long time before 'the case of the Brettergh cattle' was forgotten; but better still, a long time before Catherine's happy death was forgotten. And there were many such deaths in those days. The Reformation grew and dark Lancashire became Protestant in spite of the seminaries, the Canaanites still in the land.

Mistress Ratcliffe

MISTRESS Ratcliffe used to think that the happiest thing in life was to watch a play. Her home was in Chester, and she would go either to the High Cross or to the Rood Eye, or even into one of the very churches, to watch a play; some old popish play it would be, with the actors taking the part of holy men of the Bible, and *acting* the stories about them.

Poor Mistress Ratcliffe! no one with the fear of God would delight in that, but dancing and watching plays were her chief pleasures.

I wonder if her husband was any relation—grandson perhaps—to old Ralph Ratcliffe of Cheshire. If so, perhaps it was no wonder that they thought about plays a great deal; Ralph had left a great name behind him amongst lovers of plays, because he had gone down from Cheshire to Hitchin, and turned an old monastery into a grammar school, and (just as if he had been living today) was always inviting the neighbours to come and watch the boys acting.

Well, "she that liveth in pleasure is dead while she liveth" (1 Tim. 5, 6). But God had mercy on Mistress Ratcliffe and

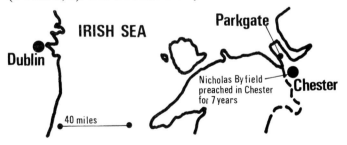

IRISH SEA

Dublin

Parkgate

Nicholas Byfield
preached in Chester
for 7 years

Chester

40 miles

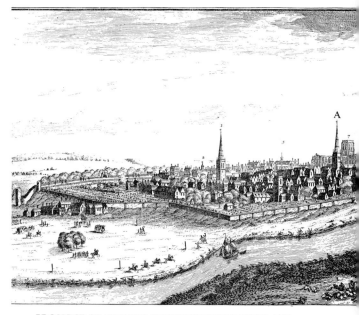

PROSPECT OF CHESTER FROM THE SOUTH-WEST, 1728.

gave her a new heart. "It pleased God," the old story says, "according to His election of grace, in due time to call her by the ministry of Mr. Nicholas Byfield."

Mr. Byfield, I should think, heard enough about plays and dramas in his life; his old home where his father had been Rector was Stratford-upon-Avon, the home of William Shakespeare who was living at the same time. It was not however that gay young Mistress Ratcliffe tripped down into Warwickshire or anything of that kind, but that Mr. Byfield went to Chester. He was on a journey to Ireland where he hoped he might be set up over a congregation. For years in the Middle Ages it was from Chester that people sailed to Ireland, and in Mr. Byfield's time, 1608, it was from a new little place, New Quay (now Parkgate) a few miles from the old city. Sandbanks were filling the River Dee very much at Chester, and so the ships had to be in deeper water nearer

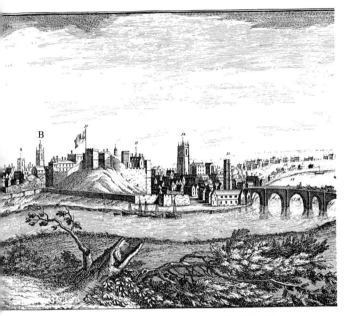

A—St. Peter's Church; B—St. Michael's.

the estuary to spread their sails. But a full tide was not the only thing required—there could be no sailing unless a favourable wind sprang up and to be "waiting for the wind at Chester" was one of the commonest experiences that passengers to Ireland had in those days.

So there was Mr. Byfield windbound, and that for so many days that he had time to preach over and over again. God blessed his preaching so much to the people that they pressed him to stay as their 'lecturer', and he did not go to Ireland at all but stayed in Chester and preached in St. Peter's church for seven years! The Chester people thought that was a *change for the better*. Mistress Ratcliffe was one of his hearers. But oh! she had never heard preaching of that kind before; all her pleasure in dancing and plays was turned unto misery. "What will ye do in the end thereof?" (Jeremiah 5. 31) was her feeling. At the same time her baby died, her

ST. PETER'S CHURCH, CHESTER

first-born, and she felt that God was against her. Sometimes, the story says, her pangs were so terrible that it was a difficult thing to fasten any comfort upon her. But God, who only can comfort a soul whom He has in mercy wounded, quieted her troubled spirit, and let her know that He loved her and had forgiven her sins for Christ's sake; and while she felt that she forgot her poverty and remembered her misery no more. Time went on, and she often looked so light-hearted and happy in the midst of all kinds of loss (because of "finding unspeakable comfort" in praying to God) that worldly people looked at her with a kind of awe.

Mr. Ratcliffe was Mayor of Chester in 1611. One day he brought home a dress for his wife to wear that was so much grander than she liked that she implored him to excuse her from wearing it. I wonder if it was all over tinsel and embroidery; perhaps it had fifteen yards of cloth in it; some of the Court Ladies' dresses had nineteen yards! Mr. Ratcliffe wanted her to wear it, however, and she did so, partly because it was no grander than many other ladies wore and partly because she would never have dreamt of not obeying her husband.

ST. PETER'S, CHESTER

Mr. Ratcliffe was a good Mayor; in his year he put an end to the custom of reapers coming to the market square on the Lord's day in harvest time to be hired for work for the following week. Twice he was Mayor and for some time he was a Member of Parliament. He died, and Mistress Ratcliffe was a widow for many years. Sometimes she was a little afraid of what might happen in England, but she died in 1638 before the storm of the Civil War came on. Her face had been paralysed for some time, and "it was the shipwreck of much beauty and comeliness." What a quaint sentence!—the old story is full of quaint sentences, but there are pages and pages of Mistress Ratcliffe's praises and she would not have liked that; she felt that she was very sinful. "She shadowed herself from acquaintance with the world," but was very much loved by other godly people in Chester.

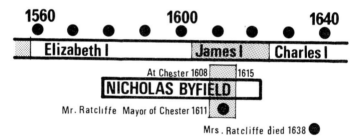

1560   1600   1640

Elizabeth I   James I   Charles I

At Chester 1608   1615
NICHOLAS BYFIELD

Mr. Ratcliffe Mayor of Chester 1611

Mrs. Ratcliffe died 1638

Prison No Prison

EVERY Saturday the work in the house of Mr. William Cook had to be finished at 5 o'clock, and the boys had to stop playing. Mr. Cook gave them a Bible lesson for an hour-and-a-half and then they went to their rooms and learned verses and the Catechism. At 8 o'clock the boys had supper with Mr. Cook; then they sang a psalm, he read and prayed, and they went to bed. There was no Mrs. Cook and the boys were not Mr. Cook's sons, but four poor boys whom he clothed, boarded and sent to school for some years. Their parents or uncles and aunts were most grateful to Mr. Cook,

ST. MICHAEL'S CHURCH, CHESTER

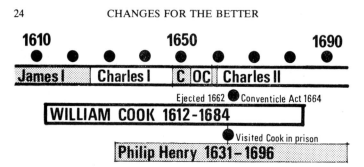

indeed his liberality was said to be stupendous, but he himself said, "I have nothing to boast of."

Mr. Cook was the assistant-minister of St. Michael's Church in Chester, but on August 17th, 1662, he told the boys that that was the last day he would be there; the next Lord's day he would have no right to stand in the pulpit. A law had been passed that all the preachers in the Church of England should declare their consent to every word in the Prayer Book, and that if they had not been ordained by a bishop they were to be so before August 24th, and if not they

ST. MICHAEL'S PORCH, CHESTER

CHESTER ROWS

must retire from their office. So Mr. Cook retired; he was one of nearly two thousand ministers who had to leave their pulpits. For twenty years the law had been on their side but now it was no longer. Sadly the congregation filed out of the church into the porch: some turned left and down the steps to ground level: others turned right along the 'Rows' for which Chester is famous. Over the shops at street level run these public passages set behind the balcony of each one's property, so making another row of shops above the others – a sort of two-level precinct. Right along the street one walks, looking across to the 'Rows' on the other side: every so often is placed a staircase of stone steps to reach the street again. You can walk along them today where all those years ago Mr. Cook's people sadly wended their way homewards.

For some months many of Mr. Cook's people met in his house for worship, but at last not without being disturbed. Those of you who have learned the history of Charles II's reign, will know that in the year 1664 the First Conventicle Act was passed. It declared that all religious meetings in houses where more than five persons besides those of the

3

PHILIP HENRY

household were present, were seditious assemblies, and all over sixteen years old who attended would be fined or imprisoned. But long before 1664 the meeting in Mr. Cook's house was broken up for a time. In those days there were some magistrates who knew that they would not get into any trouble by being more strict with the Puritans than the law was. There was another minister in that part of the country—Mr. Philip Henry—and in July 1663, not 1664, he wrote in his diary: "I went with Mr. Steel into Wirral; we called at Chester, and saw Mr. Cook, prison no prison." The mayor of Chester had taken the law into his own hands, and sent Mr. Cook to prison.

Mr. Cook minister of
St. Michaels Church, Chester
took refuge in Puddington

10 miles

I think you will understand that "prison no prison" means that Mr. Cook was no more unhappy in prison than if he had been at liberty. It was the same with him two years later when the Five Mile Act was in force—the Act which said that there was to be no house or field preaching within five miles of a town. At that time Mr. Cook took refuge in Puddington which is over five miles north-west from Chester, and he said then to his friends: "What little peace and quietness there is in the world, God's people enjoy it in their corners." Puddington is a little gem of a hamlet, still very quiet and peaceful, down a lane and in a corner, and with a view of the Welsh hills across the river Dee! Mr. Cook enjoyed being in hiding there, but he also felt free and happy in prison—how, and why?

To answer these questions it does not do to say, "A godly man is happy everywhere, he always has peace." Sometimes a godly man is unhappy—like Hezekiah who said, "For peace I had great bitterness" (Isa. 38. 17). But God says to His people: "There hath no temptation taken you but such as is common to man: but God is faithful, who will not suffer you to be tempted above that ye are able, but will with the temptation also make a way to escape that ye may be able to bear it" (1 Cor. 10. 13). It would have been harder for Mr. Cook if he had had to leave a dear wife and four little ones of his own at home. He preached to the prisoners twice a day, and had "the freeman's chamber" for his room, and visits from his friends. At Puddington it was not prison at all but a house, friends, and preaching. The rough wind was stayed in the day of the east wind (Isa. 27. 8).

But surely prison *was* an "east wind." The Lord would not say, "I was sick and in prison, and ye visited Me," if sickness and prison were nothing. Who would like to leave his home and go to the common jail for some months just at the will of a cruel mayor? and who does not know that an angry mind can spoil ever so pretty a place? The visitor, Mr. Philip Henry, who wrote "prison no prison," must have heard something from Mr. Cook that convinced him that "the Lord was with him" as He was with Joseph (Gen. 39). Mr. Cook was said to be "a man of a most godly life and unwearied labour; one of the primitive stamp, who could go in poor clothing, live on a little, travel on foot, preach and pray almost all the week when he had opportunity, in season and out of season, trampling on this world as dirt and living a mortified, laborious life." As a boy he had been a pupil of Mr. Ball*, that schoolmaster whose prayer for his children and pupils was that they might not seek great things for themselves, and who used to say that one thought of Jesus *reaching the heart* was worth more than all the comfortable, happy earthly things you could have, even if you had them all for a thousand years. His prayer was answered for his pupil William Cook; he must have had at least one thought of Jesus *reaching his heart* in prison. Perhaps it was that He was a brother born for adversity.

After Mr. Cook's day, a Mr. Armitage came to Chester, and he thought it would be a good idea to have a lecture each Thursday. Everything was arranged, but the first Thursday poor Mr. Armitage just couldn't find a text. At long last, Judges 13. 23 'came', which says, 'If the Lord were pleased to kill us, he would not...have shewed us all these things, nor would as at this time have told us such things as these.' That same night the strollers were presenting a puppet-show in the town, and some wondered whether to go to the lecture or to the puppet-show: they decided they would go to hear Mr. Armitage that evening, and go to the show another day. But that night, sad to say, a large quantity of gunpowder exploded in a room beneath the puppet-show, and forty people were killed, and many more badly burnt. Those that had gone to hear Mr. Armitage were filled with awe – now they could see what the text meant – 'If the Lord had intended to kill us, he would have permitted us to go to the puppet-show, but as He has spared us we will never go again.' And as soon as Mr. Armitage heard of it, he knew then why he couldn't find a text, and why that one 'came'. The lecture at Chester was another *change for the better*.

The Meek Mr. Langley and His Friends

HE was the minister of Middlewich in Cheshire for forty-eight years from 1609 to 1657. When he died his friends spoke of him as "holy and meek Thomas Langley," and said they had lost a friend and father in him. His trials, whether inward or outward, were made a blessing to him and God gave him a meek and quiet spirit.

The first mention of him is in 1625. One day in January that year he and his friend William Hinde, the minister of Bunbury, met at the manor-house of Bruen-Stapleford. John Bruen, the Puritan country gentleman, was on his death-bed.

MIDDLEWICH CHURCH

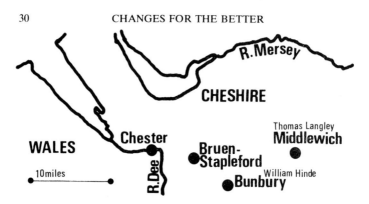

His son and heir had visited him that day, to his great joy, and he had finished praying for and blessing his son's children when Mr. Hinde and Mr. Langley arrived. The dying man was glad to see them, and told them that the Lord had, in His mercy, given him strong evidences of His favour and love in Christ.

They resolved to sit quietly by, but before long Mr. Langley spoke about death being no terror to him, and Mr. Bruen responded in a clear cheerful voice. This did not surprise them; they had heard from the family that he had lately had some such views of God and glory that he could not be prevailed upon to make them fully known. The two friends were going to stay the night, and Mr. Bruen asked Mr. Hinde to conduct the evening prayers in 'the great parlour,' and leave the door of the little parlour open so that he might hear.

Mr. Langley had to go a very long journey on horseback the next day to preach a "Reformation lecture," so he rose very early in the morning, perhaps four o'clock; any later hour would not in those days have been called very early. It was not too early however for his dying host; he wished to drink with him before parting, and a hot posset* was brought. It was customary to drink to each other's health and men of God like these made it an opportunity of praying for each other. Mr. Langley prayed for Mr. Bruen, and left the manor house on that cold dark morning warm with the thought of his friend's prayer for him.

*posset = Hot milk curdled with wine.

BUNBURY CHURCH

The next day Mr. Bruen died, and Mr. Hinde the other friend went sorrowfully to his home; his feeling was like David's when Abner died, viz.: "Know ye not that there is a prince and a great man fallen this day in Israel?" He wrote his life, and in it he tells that when John Bruen was a young man, in the days of Queen Elizabeth, there was scarcely a town or village in the county of Cheshire that possessed a minister who knew anything of the Bible. They were ignorant, lazy, popish priests, who had turned Protestant in name only, to obey the law, and Mr. Bruen's searching out men of God and inviting them to preach was the means of a great and blessed change, which began in his own village and spread through the whole country. Mr. Hinde had heard him say that when first he began to profess religion, he was like an owl of the desert, his enemies were mad against him, popery and profanity were so rife. But at the end of his life he said, "Blessed be God, every quarter and corner of the country is now filled with the sweet savour of the gospel." A *change for the better* had come to the land.

Mr. Hinde had come to Bunbury in 1603; he died in 1629 and Mr. Langley buried him, preaching from the words, "Do they not err that devise evil? but mercy and truth shall

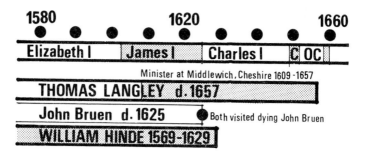

be to them that devise good" (Proverbs 12.22).* He was one who had suffered for ignoring the *Book of Sports.* He had to pay a heavy fine and was suspended from his ministry for some years. He was in the diocese of Bishop Moreton whom the king caused to draw up that ungodly book, and who was therefore eager to enforce it. At the Bunbury Wakes they had bull and bear-baiting, and at Midsummer they leapt over St. John's fires, an old heathen custom. Against these and Sabbath sporting Mr. Hinde had set his face. He had not however seen at Bunbury such a reformation as the Squire John Bruen had seen at Stapleford.

Mr. Bruen's custom had been to make these days an occasion for entertaining at his bountiful table whoever liked to come, while his chaplain *Mr. Sabbath Clark,* and two ministers from a distance preached three times. Mocking jeers met the first comers; but by God's blessing these days became times of refreshing from the presence of the Lord. Numbers were converted. Mr. Bruen had mills in Chester and could afford to be a Gaius (see 3 John verse 1) all the year round, and other squires in England were like him. The high church party did not like it and in course of time came Archbishop Laud's law that no untitled person (like *Mr.* Bruen) might have a private chaplain. Sabbath Clark had many souls for his hire.

The Reformation lectures, one of which Mr. Langley preached that day before Mr. Bruen died, were hated also by persecuting high churchmen. In 1631 he, with others who preached these lectures, was silenced. He was kept from his own pulpit for five or seven years. But someone with a title,

*The old version

Lady Bromley, received him to her house and he found work for his whole time. What could Satan do to stop the spread of the gospel? It was like Bunyan's man pouring water on to the fire while a man behind the wall was pouring oil on to it.

When Mr. Langley himself was an old man, Simeon Ash came to have a talk with him. Simeon was a minister too, and was well-known in London, but as a boy he had had a very strict upbringing: always being 'kept down' so, he drooped under it sadly, and all his life tended to be downcast. On this occasion he happened to be under some discouragement, and said to Mr. Langley that he might drop into heaven shortly. Straightway Mr. Langley replied, 'Speak sense, man; do folks usually drop upwards?' So Mr. Langley tried to be like the man in Ecclesiastes 4. 10 who 'will lift up his fellow,' and he was like it all through his life.

There is just room for a little more about Simeon Ash. He was born at Ashby in 1597 during Mr. Hildersham's time, and in his early teens he went to the church at Calke, just two or three miles away, to hear Mr. Herring, of whom you will hear more later. Calke is in lovely countryside with hills and woods, and today there is a little reservoir in the valley below. What Simeon heard that day went straight to his heart like an arrow, and convinced of being a sinner *against God*, it was such a trouble to him he could not describe it. But he came to know what could *relieve* it, and through God's blessing on the gospel he heard, he was given joy and peace in believing in Jesus Christ the Saviour.

Hardly a year later it was time for him to go up to Emmanuel College, Cambridge: and being from a poorer family he became a 'sizar', which meant he did all the domestic little jobs for another student instead of paying the full amount. He would live with the other student, and probably his bed would be a truckle-bed, like a camp-bed, that would slide away under the main bed. The older man he served had not long become an M.A., and his name was Thomas Hooker. But there came a day when Thomas was in trouble such as he had never known before: he too was convicted of being a sinner against God. Oh the trouble in his mind and heart. He couldn't sleep, tossing and turning on his bed all night long.

Simeon gently asked what was the matter. Thomas replied, "I can compare with any man living for fears." Being together in their room they were both able to say what was going on in their very heart and soul, and Simeon was used by the Lord to bring comfort to him in his distress. Thomas was later to have an eventful life as a minister before him, but after college Simeon himself returned to begin his ministry in Mr. Ball's neighbourhood (see page 87). They became so friendly that Mr. Ball left him all his manuscripts when he died, and Simeon was able to publish some of them. In the times of the Civil War, Simeon was present as a chaplain at the Battle of Edghill on the parliament side: they designed to rest on the Lord's Day but the Royalist troops forced the engagement. He lived most of his life as a minister in London, where he died 20th August 1662, being buried on the very eve of the Great Ejection. Before he died, he said, "When I think of Christ, I have enough: He is all and in all. It is one thing to *speak* of Christ and heaven, and another thing to *feel the consolation* of Christ and heaven, *as I do.*"

In his will he left a legacy to his native town, Ashy de la Zouch, Leics., for twelve pence worth of bread to be given in bread every Sunday to the poor – did he remember his Sundays at Calke? – and four Bibles to be given each year to poor people. So his good work went on after he was gone. May the Lord bless us with the *consolation* of the gospel he felt. Read the beginning of Philippians chapter two, and may the secret of the Lord be given you.

The Warming Pan

WHEN we want to warm the sheets in these days, we use either hot water bottles, or electric blankets. Long ago people used copper warming pans and they are often hanging up for sale in antique shops. People buy them, but only hang them up for ornaments, perhaps in the hall, and the warming pan looks brightly down as much as to say, "What *me* in the hall, instead of doing hard work and being in the kitchen! Well, I know you have cleverer ways of doing things nowadays, but while I am hanging up here I must tell you a story of long ago."

The way of using copper warming pans was this:—the lid was lifted, coals or cinders or charcoal, all red hot, were put in and the lid was locked firmly down; the warming pan was carried up to the bed and pushed backwards and forwards all over the sheet, or else left as we leave the hot water bottles. I think however that it was pushed about just before the bed was to be used. That was the way in any case when Mr. Carter was going to sleep.

It is a long time since Mr. Carter was living—three hundred years. When Mr. Carter had gone to be ordained, the bishop asked him, "Have you read the Bible through?" "Yes," Mr. Carter said, "I have read the Old Testament

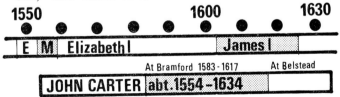

1550   1600   1630

E M Elizabeth I   James I

At Bramford 1583 - 1617   At Belstead

JOHN CARTER abt. 1554 – 1634

JOHN CARTER

twice through in Hebrew, and the New Testament often through in Greek; and if you please to examine me upon any particular place, I will try to satisfy you." "No," said the bishop, "if that is the case, I need say no more." And so he commended and encouraged him to the ministry. He was a good minister and lived at Bramford near Ipswich for many years from 1583 to 1617. He and Mrs. Carter had nine children, John, Eunice and seven others, and the people in the congregation loved them all very much. But Mr. Carter was poor, and he and Mrs. Carter wore such old-fashioned

BRAMFORD CHURCH

clothes that rude strangers would laugh and say, "Oh! I saw Adam and Eve today." They had only wooden plates (called trenchers) and dishes and a little old black wooden salt-cellar for every day uses, but a few pewter dishes for best; pewter was cheap then, and if you had only pewter and no silver you were thought to be really poor. On the Lord's day nobody stayed at home but the dinner was always left cooking; perhaps you do that; it is a good plan. They left a piece of meat simmering in a pot that hung over the fire, and in the pot was a pudding, very likely a Suffolk dumpling.

A poor man once met Mr. Carter and started telling him such a sad tale. "Mr. Carter, what will become of me? I *work* hard and *eat* well, but I don't get on." "Oh," said Mr. Carter, "there's one thing missing. You must work hard, and fare hard, and *pray* hard, and then you will be sure to get on."

Once he stole up behind one godly workman who was tanning hide – a very smelly, messy job – and Mr. Carter tapped him on the shoulder. The man was so startled, and coloured up, saying, "I am ashamed that you should find me like this." Mr. Carter answered, "Let Christ, when He cometh, find me so doing." The man could hardly believe his ears; "What," he said, "doing this?" "Yes," Mr. Carter replied, "faithfully performing the duties of my calling."

Now for the copper warming pan. Once he was invited to preach at a place in cold weather. It was not near Bramford, and he was to stay at a house all night, and the old story says that while the servant was warming his bed Mr. Carter talked to her in such a way that she could never forget the night. It made her think that she was not ready to go to heaven if she died. She had never thought about her soul before, but God blessed her, and that was "the beginning of days" to her soul, *a change for the better.*

Mr. Carter always was kind, gentle and friendly with servants. On that cold night, you see, he did not go into the room and think to himself, "Now be quick; this might have been done before I came." Very likely the mistress wanted Mr. Carter's bed to be as cosy as it could be, and if the sheets were made of very coarse linen and the bed very large (as beds often were) they would 'strike cold.'

When Mr. Carter died (Mrs. had died a good long time before him), John and Eunice had some very loving things said to them at the funeral and it was then that the servant told Eunice about Mr. Carter having talked to her. She said that his talk was "heavenly."

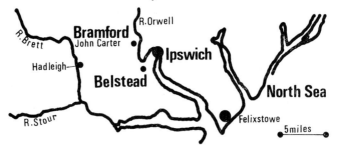

Milk for Children

HISTORY contains a picture of Mr. Carter in his old age. He lived alone with his daughter Eunice. Eunice, though she loved him very much, addressed him as "Sir." If she had said, "Father," it would have been better, but she was only doing as other daughters in those days did.

Mr. Carter had had to leave Bramford, the place of his first ministry, because of the malice of some powerful men, and he lived from 1617 to 1634 just a few miles away at Belstead in the country, preached and wrote several books. One book he called *Milk for Children*. His mind went back

BELSTEAD CHURCH

to the days when all his children were about him, and to the Saturdays at Bramford, when every week the children of the poor people came to his house with jugs, cans, and bowls, and had them filled for nothing. Mr. Carter had one or two cows of his own, but kept none of the Saturday milk, and the children used to love to go round to the dairy and have their jugs filled by Mistress Eunice or Mistress Mary, and have a smile or a kind word from them. But although Mr. Carter remembered about the milk and the Bramford children, the milk of his book was of another kind. It was what the Bible calls, "the sincere milk of the Word"—the Scriptures themselves. The book was a catechism for children—first question, then answers. It was one of the commonest things in Puritan times for ministers to write catechisms for children; at last one was composed by a number of ministers who all met together at Westminster in 1643, and that one has lasted to this day, and is still learned (though perhaps in Scotland only) by very many children. The questions and answers are of this kind:-

Question. What is God?
Answer. God is a Spirit infinite, eternal and unchangeable, in His being, wisdom, power, holiness, justice, goodness and truth.

Mr. Carter's last message to his children was, "Stand fast in the faith and love one another." He was preparing to go to preach one Sabbath morning in February 1643, when he felt faint, asked Eunice to lead him to his bed, and lying down at once fell asleep in Jesus.

Another story was about Mistress Ratcliffe of Chester, whose baby died, and whose heart was opened by the Lord to attend to the preaching of Mr. Byfield*. Mistress Ratcliffe had an uncle Mr. Edward Brerewood, who was the first Professor of Astronomy at Gresham College, London. He was one of those men of genius who will undergo any hardship for the sake of learning, so poor while at the university, that he could not for a long time venture out of his room, because of his ragged appearance. Now this genius waged war in writing with Mr. Byfield, not about the stars but about the Sabbath Day. The pamphlets they wrote are

*chapter 3, page 19.

still available in a few libraries. Mr. Brerewood was a worldly man and contended that it was right to play games on the Lord's day. Mr. Byfield contended for 'a holy resting all that day,' from work, 'except works of necessity and mercy;' and he shewed that the Word of God forbids 'such recreations as are lawful on other days.' Recreations like rest may fit us for work, but not for worship. In the book of Isaiah God speaks of 'Not doing thy pleasure on My holy day.' These words, 'a holy resting,' etc., are not Mr. Byfield's exact words, but they are his meaning. They are the words of the Westminster Catechism. The Westminster ministers, or divines, all knew Mr. Byfield's pamphlets about the Sabbath; they had made a great stir in the whole country, and his son Mr. Adoniram Byfield sat with them as their secretary. We would not have had our quiet Sabbath days in England if there had been no men like Mr. Carter, Mr. Bains, Mr. Byfield and the Westminster divines. The 'milk' dealt out by them made their children grow, and blessed were the *poor* children who, having no money, went and bought it—"milk, without money and without price" (Isaiah 55. 1).

You remember another story was about Paul Bains,* whose speech before the Privy Council so awed his judges that they dismissed him, one of them saying, "He speaks more like an angel than a man." Mr. Bains was once staying at the house of his sister-in-law Mrs. Sheafe in Cranbrook, and noticed that she was fond of card-playing. To *chess* he had no objections, but to card-playing many, and he took occasion to speak against it in his sermon on the following Sabbath. This might have made Mrs. Sheafe very angry. Indeed she asked him afterwards why he had not spoken to her about it at home, but she was in tears not in anger. "Oh," she said, crying, "why did you let me live in such sin and leave me so to dishonour God?" Mr. Bains replied that she might not have listened to him, and that it was best that God had wrought upon her by the public ministry. She was convinced of the sin of it and never returned to it.

Several times in these pages you have read of the Westminster Assembly of divines, and I must explain that in 1643 the Parliament ordered that the best-known ministers

*Volume 1, page 113.

from all parts of the country, and some from Scotland too, should meet to decide on the right way to worship God in the national churches. To tell you about the interesting lives of all the ministers who met would need another book: they included Dr. Robert Harris of Hanwell, Dr. Staunton, Simeon Ash, Herbert Palmer of Ashwell, and Henry Scudder whom you will read of in these pages. Good Lord Wharton was there as well.

One of the things they did that has lasted down the years is the Catechism that they made, to teach families and children by question and answer the main truths of the gospel. It is still called the Westminster Catechism, after the place where the ministers met. Each one had to promise and vow in the presence of Almighty God, to maintain nothing in doctrine but what was agreeable to God's word, and nothing in discipline but what was most for God's glory and the peace and good of the church. What excellent aims they were! may we today have the same aims and purpose.

Holy Mr. Dod

FLAVEL'S *Divine Conduct, or the Mystery of Providence,* is one of the sweetest and simplest books of our puritan heritage. The words, "He reached her parched corn, and she did eat," were true literally when Ruth, gleaning in the fields of Boaz, sat at his table at mealtime, "and was sufficed, and left." And they are often true figuratively. Such a book as *Divine Conduct,* preserved all these years, has often been a spiritual feast to those who through grace have grown tired of modern heathenish literature. Before they have finished the book they have felt satisfied that that divinity will do them good.

In *Divine Conduct* mention is made of 'holy Mr. Dod': "That holy man Mr. Dod, being late at night in his study, was strangely moved though at an unseasonable hour to visit a gentleman of his acquaintance; and not knowing what might be the design of Providence therein, he obeyed and went. When he came to the house, after a few knocks on the door, the gentleman himself came to him and asked him whether he had any business with him? Mr. Dod answered, 'No, but he could not be quiet till he had seen him.' 'Oh sir,' replied the gentleman, 'You are sent of God at this hour, for just now' (and with that takes the halter out of his pocket) 'I was just going to destroy myself.' And thus was the mischief prevented."

Twice Flavel speaks of 'holy Mr. Dod,' and the same high epithet is used by Samuel Clark when writing about the works of Richard Sibbes, whose books, *The Bruised Reed* and *The Soul's Conflict,* are still as parched corn to hungry ones in our own day. It was by 'holy Mr. Dod's' advice that his reluctance to publish his *Sermons on the Canticles* was overcome.

CHESTER ROWS

Now this holy man of God, whose own books are not so well-known as those of the men who so revered him, was looked up to as the chief among the mighty by many among them. "What would Mr. Dod say?" was a common question, and journeys were taken to ask his advice. For long years and in troublous times he served his generation. He fell asleep in 1645, but he was ninety-six years old, and so as his call by grace was in his younger years he was eminently one of the godly men of the days of Queen Elizabeth.

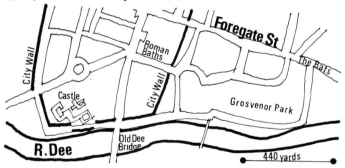

In 1571 he was twenty-two years old, and a student at Jesus College, Cambridge, a Protestant but not yet a Christian. He was the seventeenth child of his parents. His family had lived for generations 'on a fair estate' at Shocklach in the south-west corner of Cheshire not a mile from the River Dee, and as a little boy John was educated at King's School, Chester. There he must have heard and enjoyed that city's famous story, a story that must have been the delight of many little boys as well as of older ones. One night in 1558 (when John was nine years old), Mrs. Mottershed the innkeeper of the Blue Posts Inn, in the Rows in Foregate Street, had a traveller under her roof who was from Queen Mary's court in London—Master Cole, entrusted with a Commission "to destroy, to slay, and to cause to perish" (Esther 8. 11) the Protestants in Ireland. No fair wind sprang up that night to carry a ship from Chester to Ireland so that Master Cole had to wait. Now Mistress Mottershed knew about the Commission; she knew that it was in his brief-case; she had a brother in Ireland who was a Protestant and (as "there is no friend like a sister") she took an opportunity to open the brief-case, take out the Commission paper, and substitute for it a pack of cards. Next day Cole sailed for Ireland and did not discover the exchange till he was about to present the Commission. In a rage he returned for a new one, but *that* day was November 18th—too late—Queen Mary had died on the 17th, and Haman had to haste to his house mourning. Queen Elizabeth upon hearing the story, looked upon Mrs. Mottershed as so "blessed above women in the tent" that she granted her a pension of £40 a year for life.

I like to think of Cole's ship being amongst the last that sailed from Chester to Ireland, bringing its record as a seaport so sweetly to an end! It was only for about eight years more that 'the old cobbled quay' was any use; the sands of Dee were encroaching; a new quay had to be built at Parkgate, and soon Liverpool began to rival the new port. I was dining in a Chester cafe once when a troop of merry little boys from King's School came in. I noticed they all chose Irish stew. How many long years before, little John Dod and his schoolfellows had enjoyed *their* dainty Irish dish!

GOD'S PROVIDENCE HOUSE, CHESTER

The wording on the beam, 'God's Providence is mine inheritance' is a reminder of the time plague visited the city, and many inhabitants were fleeing into the country. In every street were sick, dying and dead: grass grew in the streets. The man who lived at this house felt he could trust his God who had said to him, 'There shall no evil befall thee, neither shall any plague come nigh thy dwelling' (Psalm 91. 10). Nearer the plague came until the houses either side succumbed: still he and his family trusted God. And at last when the plague slowly abated, neighbours returned to find him still happily trusting his God. And there to this day still stands this inscription which the grateful man had carved on his house to the glory of his preserving God.

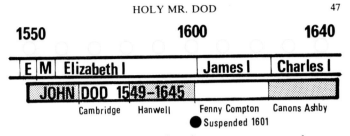

| E | M | Elizabeth I | | James I | Charles I |

JOHN DOD 1549–1645

Cambridge   Hanwell   Fenny Compton   Canons Ashby
● Suspended 1601

Mr. Dod was at college for sixteen years—a student, a tutor, and a Fellow. Samuel Clark writes of his conversion: "The steward of the college accused him to the Master for the non-payment of a considerable sum of money due for one of his pupils, which Master Dod had truly paid, but he forgot to set it down. Hereupon there was a vehement contest between them about this business, and the vexation of mind that he should be accounted a defrauder did so trouble Master Dod that he fell into a fever and was dangerously sick. Yet all this while he was but in a natural state, for though he had some good skill in the theoretical part of divinity, yet he was without any application; and his affliction was this, that he should be blamed for that which he, from the law of light and nature, hated. All his sorrow was as yet but worldly sorrow, and as himself says, he neither did nor could tell how to pray.

"At length, the Lord put into his heart that scripture, Romans 7. 14: 'The law is spiritual, but I am carnal, sold under sin'; and presently his sins came upon him like armed men, and the tide of his thoughts was turned, and he left musing how he was wronged, and seriously considered how he had offended God, and he betook himself to great humiliation, and earnestly besought the Lord for pardon and peace in Christ Jesus. Yet for some time he could find no comfort; but going on to seek the Lord there follows after much humiliation much consolation, and the Lord sealed to him that his sins were washed away with the blood of Christ." That was the vital *change for the better* we all need to feel so much.

While Dod was still at College, he went once a week to preach in Ely, "where the Lord gave a great blessing to his

JOHN DOD

ministry." Then about 1579 Sir Anthony Cope, a squire near Banbury (once chamberlain to Queen Catherine Parr), applied to the head of one of the colleges for a minister for his village—Hanwell. Dod was sent, and there he remained for more than twenty years. Hanwell is a quiet village to-day*; the Hall (to within recent years) still the residence of the Cope family. I have seen the fruit trees hanging over the garden wall, and the fruit within reach of passers-by.

* in the 1930s

Happy village, when its squire could send to the press the fruit of his pen: *Meditations on the Psalms*! I have seen a bird flitting about in little Hanwell Church; happy and blessed were they that, converted through Mr. Dod's ministry, dwelt in that house (Psalm 84. 3). The harvest was great; it was said to be hundreds of souls. In preaching his aim was to distinguish between a babe in grace and a hypocrite. And, concerning law and gospel, "Some," he said, "labour to keep men under terrors, and load them with threatenings lest they should not be humbled enough; but the Gospel works true humiliation, not the law; it arises from the sense of sin and misery, joined with the hope of mercy. The damned have terror and the sense of misery enough, but that does not humble them."

His stipend at Hanwell was at first very small. When he wanted to marry, "I can scarcely keep *myself* ," he thought. Looking out of his study window he saw a hen and chickens 'scratching for their living,' and like a flash it came to him: "The hen only lived before, and now with that family of chickens they all live." The thought gave him great freedom and pleasure; he lost no time in marrying and bringing his wife Ann Bound to Hanwell. He had twelve children, yet it was by no means through keeping every farthing to themselves that they subsisted. On the Dod crest is amongst other things a wheatsheaf, as an emblem of hospitality. And both Mr. and Mrs. Dod were eminently hospitable. Her bountiful preparation on Saturday was in view of widows and

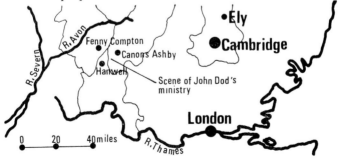

strangers who came from a distance to hear the preaching on the Lord's day. For years quite a number came from long distances, the reason being that their own ministers, ignorant and worldly men, seldom preached at all; they could not preach. In many villages the service (compulsory by law) was conducted by men whose only qualification was that they could read. Even vicious men were ordained while godly Puritans were being silenced. Then there were preachers as always whose preaching was unprofitable, and with one kind of these hirelings or another Mr. Dod was surrounded. They hated him, and in process of time they together with some in his own parish who hated him, brought him into trouble with the bishop for his strict Puritanism. Often the bishop threatened him, and once he felt these interferences and annoyances so keenly that he took a journey to Dry Drayton to unburden his mind to Mr. Greenham*. Mr. Greenham's ear, so often filled with the trouble of sin-convicted souls, was now filled with the sad tale of all the care of his buffeted friend. His answer to him was: "Son, son, when affliction lieth heavy, sin lieth light."

Mr. Dod never forgot that answer, and often afterwards he referred to it, saying, "I bless God for that answer." He had forgotten but was now reminded of his early experience, that when God spoke to him at the first, it was not till his sins came upon him "like armed men" that the affliction of losing his good name undeservedly, lay lightly. And so he went back to Hanwell. He stayed there amidst evil report and good report until nearly the end of Elizabeth's reign. Then about 1601 his enemies had their way and word came from the bishop that he was suspended, because he would not make the sign of the cross in baptism. He preached a farewell sermon to a church full of mourning people, taking for his text: "I will smite the shepherd, and the sheep shall be scattered;" Sir Anthony's power availed nothing with the bishop, and Mr. Dod with his wife and little tribe had to leave the place. They went to Fenny Compton, and there, very poor but happy, he preached till the end of the days of Queen Elizabeth—fifty-four years of his life behind, and forty-two more eventful, before him.

* See volume 1, page 77, 'Mr. Greenham's Harvest.'

When he was 62 he was taken gravely ill, and nearly died; but then the doctor began to hold out hope he *might* get better. "Oh," said Mr. Dod, "you think you comfort me by saying that, but you make me sad. It is the same as if you told a sailor, badly weather-beaten and tempest-tossed, now getting near land, that he must return to sea to be battered again by fresh winds and waves."

When he was getting older, and he felt not so strong, he usually said he was like Samson when his hair was cut: "I rise in the morning like Samson did, and think I will go out as usual; but alas! I soon find an alteration; I must stoop to old age, which has clipped my hair and taken away my strength. But I am not afraid of looking death in the face. I can say, Death, where is thy sting? Death cannot hurt me. To a wicked man death is unwelcome; but to a child of God who has laboured and suffered much, death is welcome, that he may rest from his labours."

During the Civil Wars, when some of the royalists came to his house and threatened to kill him, he calmly said, "If you do, you will send me to heaven where I long to be; but you cannot do a thing unless God give you leave." Then they broke open his chests and cupboards, taking what they liked, but he only said, 'The Lord gave, and the Lord hath taken away; blessed be the name of the Lord.' When they came back a second time, he was ill in bed, but he never said a word though they cut away the curtains from his bed and took the very pillowcases from under his head. Coming back a third time, they collected most of the household linen, and brought them into the room where he sat warming himself by the fire; while they went to look for still more, he took a pair of sheets and put them under the cushion he was sitting on; and after they had gone, he was very pleased with himself, that he had plundered the plunderers, and by a lawful robbery saved so much of his own property.

These are some of the things he used to say: "Sanctified afflictions are spiritual promotions." "I have no reason to complain of any crosses, because they are the bitter fruit of sin. Nothing shall hurt us but sin; and that shall not hurt us if we can repent of it. And nothing can do us good but the love and favour of God in Christ; and that we shall have if we seek it in good earnest."

"Afflictions are God's potions, which we may sweeten by faith and prayer; but we often make them bitter by putting into God's cup the nasty ingredients of impatience and unbelief. There is no affliction so small but we shall sink under it, if God uphold us not; and there is no sin so great but we shall commit it, if God restrain us not. A man who has the spirit of prayer has more than if he has all the world. And no man is in a bad condition, but he who has a hard heart and cannot pray." Many of his sayings have been often reprinted, and generations later could still be seen pasted on the walls of cottage rooms. An old woman told Mr. Dod himself that she would have gone distracted through the loss of her husband if she had not had his 'Sayings' in her house.

A person was once so cross at the end of his faithful preaching that he quarrelled with him afterwards, hitting him in the face so hard he knocked out two of his teeth. Without being upset, Mr. Dod spat out the teeth and blood into his hand, and holding them out said, "See here, you have knocked out two of my teeth without any provocation; but on condition I might do your *soul* good, I would allow you to dash out all the rest." So he was not overcome of evil, but overcame evil with good.

So he came to his end, beloved by his people; his enemies could only nickname him Faith and Repentance, because he preached so often of those themes. His last words were, "I desire to be dissolved and to be with Christ." So he finished his course and received the crown of righteousness in 1645, aged 96, and he was buried in Fawsley church in Northamptonshire.

Robert Balsom's Deliverances

DURING the Civil War, the king's party besieged Wardour Castle in Wiltshire, and for a long time no provision carts might approach the gates. The castle inmates had dairy produce only, but even that grew scant and starvation threatened them. But one morning a herd of swine came to the gates and they took them in; another time rabbits, and another time deer, never there before, were on the lawn. And so with pork, rabbit and venison, hunger was staved off for a time and the governor of the castle, with his family and chaplain Mr. Balsom, thanked God for the unlooked-for provision. Then the king's party besieged the castle more closely, determined that if any other such means of sustenance came, they and not the castle party would have it. But some of the soldiers declared that it was by witchcraft that the pigs, deer and rabbits had come—a minister was in the castle and he must be a wizard, or how else could the animals have arrived without the soldiers seeing them and driving them into their own camp? They did not seem to know that it was God who caused them to come.

But there is nothing too hard for the Lord and He had other wonders to show. You will hope perhaps that they were of the same kind and that the castle never had to surrender. But they were of another kind; the castle had to surrender and the officers came to make a treaty with the governor about it. While the treaty was under discussion Mr. Balsom was walking on the castle roof, and heard three soldiers say that they had sworn to take the life of one man in the castle. He asked them who that man was. "The minister," they said, not knowing that it was the minister himself to whom they were speaking. They told him that the minister had provided the castle with food by witchcraft, and they were determined to kill him.

After the treaty was made, soldiers marched into the castle and among other prisoners Mr. Balsom was taken and shut up in a low room. The key was given to the three soldiers. "The minister is in that room," they were told, "keep him safe till to-morrow morning." At night silence reigned. Mr. Balsom did not know that his keepers were the three soldiers, and they did not know even yet that the minister was the very one to whom they had spoken on the roof. At midnight they took a light, opened the door, and there they were—the good minister and the three ruffians!

How terrified Mr. Balsom must have been! Was he? *No*, "the righteous are bold as a lion"; the men were terrified. And why? It was three against one, and they would know that Mr. Balsom could not fight them all. But they were terrified because the terror of God was upon them. God sometimes strikes wicked men with a dreadful fear, and these men stood trembling and shaking, unable to lay a hand upon Mr. Balsom, while he on his part was calm and said, "Well, friends, what is your business? are you not the men who were going to take my life?" And they cowered before him and did him no harm.

The expression 'the terror of God' is in the thirty-fifth chapter of Genesis; "And they journeyed; and the terror of God was upon the cities that were round about them, and they did not pursue after the sons of Jacob." It is easy with God to disappoint "the devices of the crafty so that their hands cannot perform their enterprise" (Job 5. 12).

Well, those soldiers did no more then than offer to help him to escape! but though he thanked them, he refused to do so, saying, "I will rather the utmost that God will suffer them to inflict on me, than risk the lives of those who have showed themselves friendly." So you see, he was still looking up to his God. To show their sorrow for him, the soldiers brought him out to the fresh air, cleaned his room, and then left him.

When morning came a council of war was held and Mr. Balsom was about to be condemned to death as a rebel, but

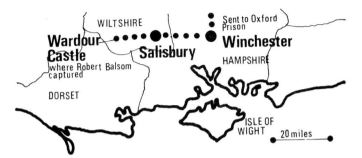

one officer said, "I will have no hand in the blood of this
man." He rose, went from the table, and the others paused.
Mr. Balsom was sent instead to Salisbury jail in a cart, the
loungers at the prison gate jeering as he was driven through.
Here he was condemned by another council of war to be
hanged at six o'clock the next morning. And so he was like a
drowning man, washed ashore but sucked back by the
retreating waves. At six o'clock a rider posted up saying that
Sir Ralph Hopton had sent a reprieve and Mr. Balsom was to
go to him to Winchester. "Mr. Balsom," said Sir Ralph, "I
little thought one day that you should have been my
prisoner, and I cannot but wonder that such men as you
should be engaged in a rebellion against the king." "Sir,"
said Mr. Balsom (for they were old acquaintances), "I
cannot but wonder that such men as you should call this
rebellion," and then they had a long talk, and after a day or
two he was sent to Oxford in charge of kind musketeers who
would allow of no rough treatment to their prisoner. He was
permitted to preach in Oxford prison and in two months was
released: how thankful he was for this *change for the better.*

Sir Ralph had at first felt: "How can any man who fears
God take sides against the king? is it not written: 'Fear God.
Honour the king'? (1 Pet. 2. 17)." And he was right, kings
must be honoured. But "he that is first in his own cause
seemeth just, but his neighbour cometh and searcheth him."
Mr. Balsom was on the side of the parliament; the
parliament had said that, "The advisers of the king are

wicked men, they tell him that he is above the law; fawning flatterers give him evil counsel about everyday affairs, and oppressors like Laud about religious affairs, and above all Jesuits lurk near his Majesty; their evil counsel and their popish arms will bury us under the hell of Rome, if we the parliament do not resist them. What are we here for? is it not to preserve the liberties of the people?" And Sir Ralph heard Mr. Balsom's side and saw that he was not one of those condemned in the Word of God, who "despise dominion and speak evil of dignities" (Jude 8). The fear of God never leads to that.

Mr. Balsom afterwards settled at Berwick where he carried on his beloved preaching. It is said he scarcely ever preached a sermon without it being the means of converting some poor wandering sinner to God. So his people loved him, God smiled on his labours, and he saw the Lord's work prospering under his hands.

He decided he would like to visit his native county of Somerset; but news came back to his waiting anxious people that he had been taken ill and had died. It was a great loss to them, but great gain to him.

In the
Vale of the Red Horse

OUR last story of Mr. Balsom and his perils in the Civil War shows how sad a state our country was brought into in those days. If you learn about the Civil War at school you may find it hard to remember the dates of the various battles—who won and what happened next; and that is partly because there is so much to be recorded that each event is summed up in a few words. I have taken a history book from the shelf, and I see that the story of the first battle for instance, is summed up in a short paragraph saying little more than that "Charles raised his standard at Nottingham and the parliamentary forces organised under the leadership of the Earl of Essex first met the royalists in the Vale of the Red Horse, at Edgehill in Warwick (Oct. 23rd, 1642); the Lords Wilmot and Aubigny were slain and the battle was indecisive." But very different from reading and forgetting that, was it to live in the midst of it!

October 23rd 1642 was a Sabbath day. Samuel Clark, in whose books I have found nearly all these Puritan stories, had invited Richard Baxter to preach to his congregation that

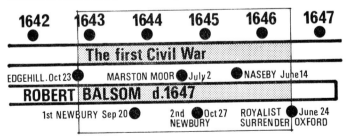

1642	1643	1644	1645	1646	1647

The first Civil War

EDGEHILL.Oct 23   MARSTON MOOR July 2   NASEBY June 14

ROBERT BALSOM d.1647

1st NEWBURY Sep 20   2nd Oct 27 NEWBURY   ROYALIST SURRENDER June 24 OXFORD day, and Baxter wrote: "On October 23rd, 1642, little knowing what was doing at Edgehill, I was preaching in his pulpit at Alcester on these words: 'The kingdom of heaven suffereth violence, and the violent take it by force.' My voice hindered me, but the auditors heard the cannon. That night was passed by us in sad watching, with the noise of the fugitive troops. The next day (such spectacles being rare and sad) Mr. Clark and I rode to the field to see what was done, where we saw the dead bodies of English men slain by one another."

The fugitive troops were those of the parliamentary army going in the evening and through the night to Coventry, which town was friendly to them. The king's troops "drew off" towards Oxford. Dr. Harris the minister at Hanwell, a village four miles from Edgehill, had preached that day. "Yet it pleased God," said Mr. Clark, "so to order it (which he, Dr. Harris, took for a great mercy) that he heard not the least noise of it (the wind sitting contrary) till the public work of the day was over, nor could he believe the report of a battle, till a soldier besmeared with blood and powder came to witness it." The public work of the day was, of course, divine service in the church morning and afternoon. For sixty years the village of Hanwell under John Dod and Robert Harris had had a faithful ministry, and at this time there was scarcely a household which did not raise its morning and evening psalm of praise. It was just such a village as the kings troops shouting "Down with the Roundheads" delighted to disturb. Often soldiers were billeted in Dr. Harris's house; generally the officers were civil and gentlemanly in and to his family, but once a company of such swearers and blasphemers came that he took for his text: "Above all things, my brethren, swear not" (James 5. 12). This made them so angry that they swore they would shoot him if he preached again from the same text. Undismayed by their threats, he ventured to preach from the same words the next Lord's Day; and as he was preaching he saw a soldier preparing his firelock ready to shoot; still Mr. Harris went on without fear, and finished his sermon without being interrupted. Yet still they threatened him; they attended his

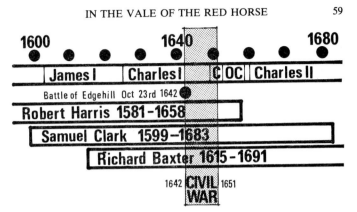

1600 ● ● ● ● 1640 ● ● ● 1680

| James I | Charles I | C | OC | Charles II |

Battle of Edgehill Oct 23rd 1642 ●

Robert Harris 1581-1658

Samuel Clark 1599-1683

Richard Baxter 1615-1691

1642 **CIVIL WAR** 1651

family prayers but scoffed because he prayed in the family without a book. At last the neighbouring woods were burned, the very houses were burned, and Dr. Harris was forced by a king's officer to leave the place.

I must tell you a little more about Dr. Robert Harris. He was appointed to preach for the very first time at Chipping Campden in the county in which he was born. When he came to the church, no Bible could be found! Some said he must ask the vicar at his house; but as it had not been seen even *there* for many months, it was very difficult to find it; at length it was discovered, and off went Dr. Harris in triumph, carrying the rediscovered treasure into the pulpit, and preached gladly from the first verse of Romans 10.

Well now, you read how Mr. Dod was 'silenced' at Hanwell, and had to leave. The good man who had to arrange for the next minister asked Dr. Harris; but the people only wanted their dear Mr. Dod to come back; so as long as there was the slightest hope of having him again, they would just listen to Dr. Harris in the meantime, while they were waiting!

But in the end it was evident Mr. Dod would not return, and strange to say, in time they grew to like Dr. Harris almost as much! Dr. Harris used to say a preacher had three books to study: the *Bible, himself* and *his people*.

When he was poorly in his last illness, he said to his friends; "You must put on all the armour of God, and then go forth in the strength of the Lord. Stand in the fight, and the issue will be glorious; only forget not to call in the help of your General. Do all from Him and under Him." He derived all his comfort 'from Christ and the free grace of God.' Someone suggested he could take comfort from what he had done for the Lord – he replied, "All is nothing without a Saviour. Without Him my best works would condemn me. Oh! I am ashamed of them, being mixed so much with sin. Oh! I am an unprofitable servant. I have not done anything for God as I ought. Loss of time sits heavy upon my spirit. Work, work fast. Be sure nothing will trouble you when you come to die, than that you have done no more for God, who has done so much for you."

What were his friends to do for him now he was dying? "You must not only pray for me, but praise God for His unspeakable mercy to me. I never saw the worth of Christ, nor tasted the sweetness of God's love, as I do now. O how good is God! Entertain good thoughts of Him. I am now going home, even quite spent. I am on the shore, but leave you still tossing on the sea. Oh! it is a good time to die in." So he went to be with his Lord, on 11th December 1658 aged 80.

Robertus Harris

Banbury Zeal

IN the last story you read of the trouble that came to the village of Hanwell after the battle of Edgehill. But on that sad October night, war-stained soldiers who took up their lodging with Dr. Harris's parishioners were mere stragglers. Hanwell was nothing to the Army compared with *Banbury* (and even Banbury nothing compared with Oxford, and Oxford nothing compared with London). The royalists might have been the victors if they had had as much success throughout as they had at Banbury, for they took the castle there. There was a saying in Oxfordshire, "Give me Banbury zeal, Banbury cheese and Banbury cakes." It was strange to mix zeal with cheese, but we are told it had once been Banbury 'veal'. On one occasion someone wrote in the town records 'zeal' by mistake and others said, "Let it stand," and laughed. The laugh was in derision because there were many *zealous* Puritans in the town. Their numbers had been increasing for about forty years. And it was a pleasing task to

some of the high-church army officers to harass and scatter the Puritan townspeople in the autumn and winter of 1642. Sad desolations, it was said, fell upon them.

I was once in Banbury. The church was open and, going in, I found in a corner a book three hundred years old. I was becoming extremely interested in its contents when it was

WILLIAM WHATELEY

time to go. The Book of Genesis was the subject; the chapters were about the earliest saints of God. Its title was "Prototype" and its preface told the reader that one Henry Scudder of Drayton had sent it to the press, but that it was the work of William Whateley who had lately (in 1639) died.

Mr. Whateley and Mr. Scudder were educated together. Mr. Scudder said, "Our tutor called all his pupils into his room every evening for prayer, and asked us to give an account sometimes of the sermons we had heard on the Lord's Day; and when any of us came to a standstill, he used to say, 'Whateley, what say you?' And away he would go, and repeat it as readily as if he had preached the sermon himself; but while this made our tutor love and admire him, it only awakened our envy and ill-will." But afterward God called them each by His effectual grace, and gave them a new heart.

Now Mr. Whateley and Mr. Scudder were among Dr. Harris's dearest and closest friends. Both were ministers,

1580		1620		1660

Elizabeth I	James I	Charles I	OC

Born at Banbury   Preacher at Banbury for 34yrs.

W. WHATELY 1583–1639

Dr. ROBERT HARRIS 1581–1658

Studied at   Preacher at Hanwell   President of
Oxford Univ.   1614–1642   Trinity C. Oxford

and all three, with Mr. Lancaster from another neighbouring village, had been accustomed to meet and study together the Bible in the original languages Hebrew and Greek. Mr. Whateley's father had frequently been Mayor of Banbury. He himself was its minister for thirty years from 1609 to 1639. He was a great preacher and however much pressed would never leave his native town. Like Mr. Dod and Dr. Harris he always had six or seven poor old widows at his table on Lord's Day. In his early ministry he met with opposition from his fellow-townsmen but as the years went on "it pleased God to put a seal to it in the converting and building up of *thousands*." He evidently had a good clear voice for he became nicknamed the Roaring Boy of Banbury. To be made the means of such great blessing might have filled him with pride. But we are told that he had great fights with his own inward sins and great temptations of the devil.

In one sermon he recommended his hearers to put in a purse by itself a certain part of every pound of their profits from trading, to be given to those in need; he said they would find instead of secretly grudging at calls for charity, they would be looking out to see where they could show it, and be glad to find such occasions. A neighbouring clergyman came to him after the sermon, and earnestly asked what proportion he ought in conscience to give. Mr. Whateley replied, "I am not to prescribe to others. But I will tell you what I have done myself. You remember how years ago I often had to come and borrow from you ten pounds at a time. And each year I could hardly manage without it. I used to receive what should have been enough; I was not conscious of any unnecessary expense. At last I asked my family what we all did for the poor, and not being satisfied with the answer, I instantly resolved to lay aside every tenth shilling of all I got for charity; and the Lord has prospered me so well since I started, that now, if you had need, I could lend you ten times as much as I have been previously forced to borrow." So it came to pass that for many years he distributed 10% of his income to the poor; and the more he gave away, the more the Lord caused his earthly business to prosper. Just like it says in Proverbs 11. 24: 'There is that scattereth, and yet increaseth; and there is that withholdeth more than is meet, but it tendeth to poverty.' It was said that he grew in humility in his last days, and died full of heavenly speeches, his eyes looking steadfastly towards heaven.

'I, William Whateley, viccar, sett myne hand to all these, but onely against them that are presented for sitting I will give none hand' – meaning that he would take no part in proceedings against those that refused on principle to kneel at communion.

It was not on Lord's days only that Banbury church was full. From far and near they came on market days. The market-day 'lecture' was a great institution in Puritan times. Easter Tuesday and Tuesday at Whitsuntide were great days too—not Monday; there was preaching at Hanwell then. We read in Dr. Harris's Life "On Easter and Whitsun Mondays multitudes of Christians resorted from far and near as the doves to the windows, yet without any superstition. And on the morrow they were entertained with the great feast at Banbury by Mr. Whateley. Oh, what a fair of souls was then held at Hanwell and Banbury by these two brothers! how did religion then flourish and professors thrive like the calves in their stalls." *Changes for the better* had come.

Quite two hundred years later Mr. Philpot published one of Dr. Harris's sermons in the *Gospel Standard.**

'These two brothers' were really brothers-in-law; Mistress Harris was William Whateley's sister. For years her health was so poor that her husband was continually reminded that he might lose her. "He would often say that he had been quite spoiled, had he not thus been taken down, for young ministers know not what ground they tread on, till God lays them flat." And still, after years had past, he walked softly on her account. In his last days, she like her brother was very much buffeted by Satan. She was tempted almost to despair. Dr. Harris was thankful to notice that never once however did she blaspheme God, and never harmed herself or anyone. Satan was allowed to go so far but no farther. But nothing that either Dr. Harris or anyone else could say, no sermons, written or preached, no sympathetic conversation comforted her. The words of both brother and husband had been used by the Holy Spirit and prospered in the thing *only* whereto He had sent them. And He reserved comfort to Mrs. Harris until she was a widow.

One day, there came to Banbury a visitor all the way from Holland; he was going to stay at one of the homes here for nearly a year. When you are living in someone else's home in another land, how you keep your eyes and ears open every minute! William Teellinck was no exception. But the more he looked and listened, the more he felt God was known and loved in that home. And it made him feel his own heart and soul weren't like that, and oh how he wanted it! He joined them in their prayers, and he felt his heart grow so tender, his mind so satisfied, through God's blessing on him while he was under this roof, that when he eventually went back to Holland, he wanted his own home to be like that – and he became a minister, and he wanted his people's homes like

* X. 116, April 1844. Preached at St. Margaret's, Westminster, 1642, on Luke 18. 1-8

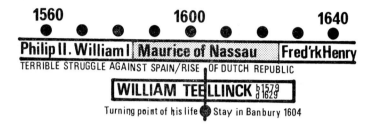

that too. Like what? – listen; he is writing a diary with one of those quill pens, and telling us what he saw.

Everyone in the Banbury home got up early in the morning, the servants too, and they all had time to pray and read, as well as getting ready for the day's work. They all went to work till noon, when all the household, old and young alike, sat down at the big table. There was the good Book, and they read together a chapter – I'm not sure whether they read round, or whether the father read it through – after which they all kneeled in prayer. Then dinner was ready! After asking for the Lord's blessing, they mentioned at the meal-table what they thought about the chapter they had just read; sometimes they had a question to answer – because if anyone had a question, and nearly everyone does have one sometimes – it was asked, and then they all thought it over for a day or two, and then over dinner, they would all say what they felt helped to answer it. After dinner was finished they sang a psalm together and then went back to work. At the evening meal it was much the same; and then when it got to bedtime, they would go over the day's events between themselves and God alone, and after supper closed the day with prayer. Sometimes they went a walk, and then they would try to have with them a friendly companion who could comment on a chapter or a psalm as they went along the leafy lanes, and it was surprising how many in Banbury seemed to have a special gift that way.

They tried to work a five-day week, finishing on the Friday

WILLIAM TEELLINCK

night, so that on Saturday they could quietly get ready and think about the next day, the Lord's Day. When the Lord's Day dawned, they all assembled, read and prayed, and all went together to the place of worship so as to get there early; oh they *did* listen well, and some even took notes, for it was the custom for them each to be asked about what they heard. William did his best, until at last he could master the English almost as well as anyone else in Banbury. So over the midday meal they discussed the sermon, and after the psalm was sung, each went to his own room to pray and think things over before going to the afternoon service. When it came to the evening, all the household gathered and went over the sermons together; the servants and children were asked questions to see how attentive they had been, and how much they had grasped; and any point that particularly applied to the family they carefully noted, and prayed to live more like the scriptures showed. So the Bible really did become to them a light to their feet and a lantern to their path.

And William keenly observed how they lived their daily lives at Banbury. The furniture in the home was marked by sturdy simplicity, their food and clothing were quite ordinary and taken care of; they were generous people, and at least once a week, usually on the Sunday, they have at least two poor godly folk for dinner. Guests were always welcome to join in their simple way of life, and were expected to take part in the daily worship. Everything was regular and orderly. The head of the house was the one who led in prayer. In business everything was straightforward; they gave to the poor, they visited anyone poorly, they educated their children – even their enemies could see the sympathy, joy, comfort and happiness that shone in their lives, to prove that the dear Lord was with them of a truth.

Shall I tell you a secret? William loved it in England; he visited different places, and fell in love with a young lady from Derby, who became his wife; and after they went back to Holland they had a very happy home of their own with a little family; and where he was the minister, the people came to love the good pastor and his faithful wife.

Drayton

WHEN I told you about Banbury zeal, the names of Mr. Scudder and Mr. Lancaster were mentioned and now we must hear something about them. There is not much to be gleaned it is true, but there is something more than merely that Mr. Scudder gathered the writings of William Whateley together, and published them in that old book which is lying perhaps even yet in a corner of Banbury church.

Mr. Whateley and Mr. Scudder married two sisters, whose

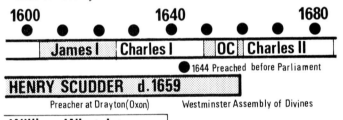

1600			1640				1680
James I	Charles I		OC	Charles II			

1644 Preached before Parliament

HENRY SCUDDER   d. 1659

Preacher at Drayton (Oxon)   Westminster Assembly of Divines

William Whately [at Banbury]

aged father George Hunt had as a young man been condemned to die at the stake; but Queen Mary, by whose desire his burning would have taken place, died and he escaped. The sisters were godly women and as you may have guessed firm Protestants. Mr. Scudder's early ministry was at Drayton not far from Banbury, and he is best known for his book, *The Christian's Daily Walk in holy security and peace*. Dr. Owen wrote a foreword to it, and said he could not remember a better book to be the daily companion of Christians, to guide them in the practice of a holy life. He heartily wished no family to be without it! It was also translated into Dutch by the scholarly Theodore Haak. Well

DRAYTON CHURCH, BANBURY, OXON.

now, Mr. Scudder's books are mentioned in the story of the life of Mrs. Elizabeth Wilkinson. She was born in Devonshire, but his books found their way there. She lived after her marriage in Oxford, at a time when Dr. Harris lived there. She told him what a comfort these books had been to her. When she was twelve years old she began to wish that she was one of God's people, but no sooner , she said, was her face turned towards Zion than she was filled with temptations that there was no God. She was in great trouble, knowing atheism to be a great sin. But, she said, the Lord had compassion on her and directed her to Calvin's *Institutes,* when the tempter left her as she was reading about the Creation. Yet, almost immediately she feared she had committed the sin against the Holy Ghost. "But the Lord directed me," she told Dr. Harris, "to the reading of Mr. Scudder's *Works,* and was pleased to satisfy my misgiving heart by a clear manifestation that I had not committed it." But another fear came; she felt she had no repentance and no faith, and perhaps was not one for whom Christ died; but then "as I was reading something in Mr. Scudder's

Christian's Daily Walk," she said, "the Lord brought my soul as much joy and comfort as I can express." These were the temptations Elizabeth had when she was between twelve and sixteen years old. She told Dr. Harris about them in writing when she was grown up, and he after her death in 1654 wrote a long warm-hearted account of her, saying, "Do not think it lost time to read over this narrative; it was penned by this gracious woman upon a serious occasion, when she was to give an account of herself at her admission to the Lord's Supper." The Lord granted that *change for the better.*

The story about Mr. Lancaster is one which I shall have to write very briefly. He was a Puritan minister near Banbury frequently silenced, and so frequently poor. "We have no money left," said his wife; "this is market-day and we need some things." "Send Martha just as usual," said Mr. Lancaster. The servant went to Banbury and her master prayed that she might have good success; she was not by any means to beg, and as the story is told as a remarkable providence we know that her master and mistress did not have a credit account; it had not been customary at the market. The maid returned with every one of the things Mrs. Lancaster wanted. First one person and then another saw her and said, "You are Mr. Lancaster's maid, are you not? Do give him this." And when "this" and "this" and "this" filled the basket, exactly as if Martha had bought them from the list given her by her mistress, there was not a friend more, and she went home surely, I think, with music in her heart.

We promised to tell you what Mr. Scudder, Mr. Bruen, Mr. Bains and the other Puritan ministers thought and taught about recreation. Mr. Scudder put it down in his book *The Christian's Daily Walk*, so we will look over his shoulder: this is what he says: 'Now that you may innocently enjoy recreation, follow these directions:

1. The *matter* of your recreation must be of a common nature, and of things of indifferent use. Things holy are too good and things vicious are too bad to be sported or played with.

2. Recreations must be *seasonable* for time, not on the Lord's Day in which God forbids all men to seek their own

pleasures, Isaiah 58. 13. Usually diversions must be used not before but *after* the body or mind has been thoroughly employed in honest business. Not overlong to the expense and loss of your precious time which you should study to redeem, not to trifle away. Ephesians 5. 16.

3.   Recreations must always be inoffensive, 1 Corinth. 16. 14, such as *do no harm* to yourself or to your neighbour. If your diversions do impeach or hazard your own or your neighbour's life, estate or comfortable living, they are unlawful.

4.   Recreation must be *moderate*, not sensual or brutish, looking at no higher or further end than earthly delights. For as he that eats and drinks that he may enlarge his appetite, to eat and drink yet more, so he who sports that he may sport is brutish and sensual. God has threatened that he who loves sport shall be a poor man, Proverbs 21. 17, and, he that loves wine and oil shall not be rich.

5.   Whatsoever your diversions are, you must recreate the outward man so that you be no worse but rather *better, in the inward man*. For God has set such a blessed order in all lawful things that the meanest being lawfully used shall not hinder but assist us in the best things.

6.   In all recreations you must *propose the right end*: the next and immediate end is to revive your weary body and to quicken your dulled mind: but your highest and principal end is that with this refreshed body and quickened spirit, you may better serve and glorify God, 1 Corinth. 10. 31, so that 'whether you eat or drink or whatsoever else you do, all may be done to the glory of God.'

Mr. Scudder thought out the truth 'as it is in Jesus' in so many ways – how to get up in the morning, how to finish each day, what sort of friends to have, what to do when we are on our own, how to be thankful, what to do in trouble, proper care and improper anxiety, false fears and true peace. No doubt his people 'heard him to profit' in the little church tucked away in the bottom of a fold in the Oxfordshire hills.

The Inn

PEOPLE were often wakened by the passing-bell, as you may suppose, when you think of it being tolled for one person at one o'clock in the morning! There is a story of its wakening Dr. Andrew Willet and his wife when they were staying at an inn in Hoddesdon in 1621.

On a dreary November afternoon ten days before, Dr. Willet had ridden up to the inn door, but had to be helped off his horse his leg was so painful. He had been thrown some miles from the inn, on his way from London to his home. The inn-keeper sent for a bone-setter who found that the leg was broken, and after setting it he ordered Dr. Willet to stay in bed ten days. That was an unexpected check in the good minister's active life; he sent to let Mrs. Willet know, and she soon came with one of their sons to keep him company until he was able to travel on. What he said to them when they entered the room is not on record, but there are two remarks, common nowadays, that I am sure he did not make.

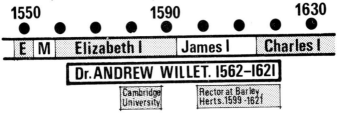

He did *not* say, with a bitter laugh: "Isn't this stupid?" or, half angrily, "This *would* happen just when I was looking forward to being at home!" Remarks of that kind would have sounded most impious in the ears of Dr. Willet. If there was

6

ANDREW WILLET

one thing more than others that he believed, it was that things do not happen without the rule and governing of God. "A man's heart deviseth his way: but the Lord directeth his steps" (Proverbs 16. 9). After two days the leg was so painful and Dr. Willet so weary that he almost felt that he would die, and he thought about Hezekiah and, as the story says, "He employed his son, who waited on him, to write from his mouth some heavenly meditations upon the story of Hezekiah when he had been sick and was recovered of his sickness."

Writing heavenly meditations was nothing new to Dr. Willet; every year he published a book and his writings were crowned with God's blessing. They have not lasted so long as Dr. Sibbes' whose books your father may have on his shelves this very day; but they were read for quite a hundred and fifty years, and the great and good Mr. Toplady praised them because they gave glory to God. The story does not say which of his sons it was who went with his mother to the inn, but the family consisted of eleven sons and seven daughters.

One son became the first mayor of New York; perhaps many of them had children of their own at that time. For a long time their home had been at Ely, and for many years that ancient school, the King's School at Ely, was not without a little Willet. And when the little Willets were at home in the evening, they still had something to learn or rather remember; and that was one verse, or even one sentence, from the chapter that was read at the evening family prayers.

Dr. Willet had had many hours of writing, and one of the children had to read while all the others and several servants sat by. Any one of them, children or servants, might be asked by Dr. Willet to repeat a verse, and he would make a few remarks about that verse before they all knelt down to pray. Some people who write a great many books take scarcely any notice of children; they think of nothing but their books; but Dr. Willet was not like that; he played with the little ones in the field behind the house, any game they liked, before dinner. If it was wet before dinner he would say, "Come and sing, children, and I will play the organ," or they would all go together to a great big shed. He would chop wood and they would pick it up, and then play an indoor game, e.g. Hoodman Blind.

He read so much, and understood and remembered what he had read so well, that people called him 'a living library'. He used to get up very early in the morning, so they said he would be halfway on his journey before the others set out.

He used to say *some* enjoyed promotions, while *others*

THE WILLET FAMILY ROUND THE ORGAN

earned them. And then, "As it is most honourable for a soldier to die fighting, and for a bishop or pastor praying; so, if my merciful God will vouchsafe to grant me my request, I desire that I may finish my days in writing and commenting on some part of scripture." And the Lord gave him the desire of his heart, for when he came to his end, he was composing his *Commentary on Leviticus.*

So you see that with his wife and children and his congregation and the people who bought and read his books, there were many people who would miss Dr. Willet when he died; and he did indeed die in that very inn, even although his illness was only the result of a broken leg. Early in the morning of the fourth of December he and his wife were awakened by the tolling of a passing-bell. They could not go to sleep again, and from the thought that somebody was dying, they began to talk about death and heaven. Somehow they both felt very happy; perhaps like the disciples on the way to Emmaus when the day was far spent and Jesus Himself drew nigh and went with them. They began to sing one of the hymns which the doctor had composed, and then the 146th psalm in metre. When they reached the words, "And loose the fetters strong," Dr. Willet said: "Oh this is a

BARLEY CHURCH

most sweet psalm; these splints on my leg are like fetters" and just then he fainted; and Mrs. Willet ran for someone to come. But though they brought water to sponge his brow, he only gave one little look saying, "Let me alone; I shall do well; Lord Jesus . . ."; and lay back, gave his last sigh and passed away. They carried the body lovingly home to Barley, where he was buried in the church; where there is now a full-length statue of him praying.

After their own children had grown up, Mrs. Willet was so happy inviting poor people to share the house: "Why," she said, "now I have my children back again!"

Not many years after Dr. Willet died, there were two boys born nearby: one was named John Janeway, born in 1633 at Lilley. He got on so well at school and college, especially in mathematics and astronomy: but when he was eighteen God made him feel deeply that it was a poor thing to know so much of the heavens, and yet never arrive there; and that the greatest knowledge in the world without Christ was an empty dry business. God taught him His wonderful mercy in Jesus Christ, and it was a wonderful preparation, for he was only twenty-two when he passed away to heaven, not seeing any more 'as through a glass darkly, but face to face'.

The other boy was Thomas Vincent, born the next year at Hertford: he lived to be one of the ministers ejected in 1662 when he was only 28. You know how only three years later God visited our land with the Great Plague, and so many of the vicars in the London churches ran away, leaving the poor people without the good gospel that they needed, specially then, that Thomas felt he *must* go in spite of the danger of catching the illness, to preach to the people. He was one of those who 'hazarded their lives for the gospel's sake' in more ways than one. He was one who *loved Jesus*.

The Pickled Herring

YOU remember reading about Dr. Willet dying in an inn in Hoddesdon, where he had to stay because he had broken his leg. Shortly after those days Dr. Lambe was on a journey in Northamptonshire and he also broke his leg and had to stay in an inn. He was a bitter persecutor of the Puritans, and that very evening a Puritan whom he hated was staying at the inn. His name was Julines Herring who laboured in Shropshire. Before nightfall Mr. Herring called the company together to conduct the evening family prayers, and he prayed so fervently for Dr. Lambe that somebody asked him afterwards why he did so for so unworthy a man. Mr. Herring's answer was that the greater enemy he was to the Church of God the more need there was to pray for him. Dr. Lambe made a good recovery and went on his way.

But Mr. Herring had a greater enemy in England than Dr. Lambe, and that was William Laud the Archbishop of Canterbury. Laud loved popery and was determined to get rid of Mr. Herring in some way and once said: "I will pickle up that herring of Shrewsbury!" I think the occasion of Mr. Herring's being in the Northamptonshire inn must have been when Laud had obtained his wish and forbidden him to preach in England, and he was going to Holland. His son was with him; they went to bid farewell to 'Aunt Bowles' who lived in Bedfordshire. Uncle Oliver Bowles went with them to Yarmouth and a great heavy sailing-ship carried them over to Rotterdam in September 1637. As soon as they landed and had found an inn, they knelt down and Mr. Herring thanked God for their safe voyage. Next day they were driven in a waggon to Amsterdam; Mr. Herring was going to be the

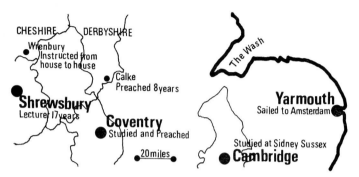

minister of a congregation of English families there, and as
they were nearing the city they were met by a company of
people—the elders and deacons of the congregation, and a
number of English merchants. They gave their new minister
and his son a hearty welcome, and took them to Master
Whittaker's house to stay until their own was ready. The next
week all the magistrates in Amsterdam came to see Mr.
Herring and then he was introduced to a company of grave
men called The Classis and a prayer-meeting was held.

One evening soon after their arrival, Mr. Herring said to
his son: "The Dutch are having a day of humiliation
to-morrow, but it would be a day of thanksgiving to me if
God would bring your mother and the children to us; come
and let us pray for them." The next morning a message came
that their ship also had arrived safely and that they were on
the road to Amsterdam. "Oh how merciful and kind God is
to me!" exclaimed Mr. Herring, and soon there was another
happy meeting, and in due time husband, wife and children
went to a house of their own and lived there to the end of Mr.
Herring's life.

I must just tell you this: toward the close of his life, and
especially the night before he died, Mr. Herring was very
sadly attacked by Satan. But no sooner was the fight with the
tempter over, and faith the conqueror, than he arose on his
knees in bed, and with his hands lifted up to heaven,
exclaimed, "He is overcome, overcome, through the
strength of my Lord and only Saviour Jesus Christ, to whom
I am now going to keep a sabbath in glory." And the next

day, a Lord's Day, he entered into the joy of his Lord, March 28th, 1644, aged 62.

What a happy thing family love is! how warm and loving it all sounds; and in *this* family story of inns and journeys, there is not the sadness that there was in the story of Dr. Willet at the inn—Mrs. Willet having to go home a widow. And yet sadness had gone before, and they knew quite well that never again would they see the faces of friends and relations they had left behind in England. Archbishop Laud had indeed "pickled that herring of Shrewsbury." To pickle a herring is to bake it with vinegar—sharp, sour vinegar—and that was what the Archbishop meant; he would deal sharply with him.

There was one old friend from whom Mr. Herring had scarcely been able to part—Mr. Ball of Whitmore. They spent a day together and talked far into the night, and prayed together. And the next day as they went together along the country road, they "parted" from each other three or four times, and yet could not part. At last, Mr. Herring on horseback on one side of a hedge and Mr. Ball walking on the other side, they kept shaking hands over the hedge and at last parted saying they would meet in heaven. Mr. Herring said that with two or three more such partings he could not have gone to Holland at all.

You may think "Herring" an amusing name, but it is an honourable name for all that; Mr. Herring's ancestors had been sheriffs and mayors of Coventry for two hundred years. His first name Julines may too sound odd, but it was a worthy name in the eyes of Mr. Herring's parents when they gave it

to him. He was named after Julines Palmer, a native of
Coventry and an Oxford Scholar, and one of the noble army
of martyrs in Queen Mary's reign.

Mr. Herring was one of those "that turn many to
righteousness" (Dan. 12. 3), and it was a solemn thing to
"silence" such a man. The historian says that there was a

CALKE ABBEY

great scarcity of good preachers, and people from twenty
towns and villages "flocked as doves to their windows" to
Calke Chapel in Derbyshire (where for eight years he
preached); the chapel could not hold all who went, and many
stood outside the windows and heard Mr. Herring's strong
clear voice. "Great companies came in the morning with
joyful expectation of wholesome soul-provisions; here they
continued all day with cheerfulness (some bringing their
victuals from home with them, and others going to a three-
penny ordinary provided purposely for the refreshing of
strangers);...and in the evening they went home in
companies, repeating the sermons and singing psalms."

Under his ministry at Calke, Mr. Simeon Ash, the godly
minister you read about on page 33, was called by God's
grace when he was in his early teens. Calke was only four

miles from Ashby-de-la-Zouch where Arthur Hildersham was, you remember*.

After his useful time at Calke, Mr. Herring had preached in Shrewsbury for a long time, but the order came, "Silence! leave your pulpit!" so he took refuge at Wrenbury, Cheshire, to live with his sister-in-law, the widow of Robert Nicholls, 'a man of clear head and tender heart': his friend William Peartree was the minister, and for a year Julines helped God's cause there by preaching from house to house: and now when he had an invitation to go to preach in Amsterdam the order was: "Watch the ports for ministers." He and his son had gone first; he had thirteen children and did not want to be recognised at Yarmouth. He was determined that if he was asked if he was a minister he could not deny it, so prayed that they would not ask him and they did not. Not only were storms and wrecks common in the North Sea but it was common for the ship to be blown back to Yarmouth. No wonder the family meeting was a happy one! A *change for the better* indeed!

WRENBURY CHURCH

*See Volume 1, page 47.

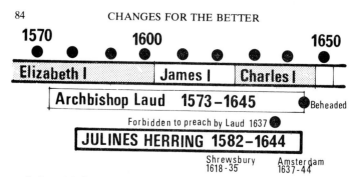

Elizabeth I James I Charles I

Archbishop Laud 1573–1645 Beheaded

Forbidden to preach by Laud 1637

JULINES HERRING 1582–1644

Shrewsbury 1618-35 Amsterdam 1637-44

It is said that whenever he corrected his children—and he had thirteen—he first tried to convince them of the evil of their sin in the sight of God, and then looked up to the Lord for a blessing on his corrections.

You read how Mr. Herring for a little time was in Cheshire at a place called Wrenbury: what happened in Cheshire after he left? Well, the Lord did not forsake His people, but raised up for them two other good ministers.

One was named John Machin: when he was twenty-four the Lord called him by His grace and he was converted, while he was in Jesus College chapel, Cambridge. Soon he was writing home to his parents and his three sisters, and I think it did them good to read what he said.

The next year 1647 he fell gravely ill: and he felt if God spared his life, he would be a preacher. The Lord restored him like Hezekiah, not for *fifteen* but just seventeen years: and having put his hand to the plough, he did not look back, saying that he saw 'the world was one long furrow', and so he kept moving on from place to place. Only three days after his marriage at Astbury, Cheshire, he set off on a preaching tour. As he journeyed about he wrote texts on walls and trees as he passed by: I am sure if he had lived today he would have loved to display posters of Bible texts wherever he could. 'The Bible was his companion in the day and his pillow at night.'

He was a man of prayer too: 'Always think of your friends with a *praying* thought', he would say.

When in 1662 he was forbidden to preach any more, he felt it was like dying; and in 1664 when he was only forty, he

CALKE CHURCH

came to his end: he told his neighbours 'he had never lived since he had died' at the Great Ejection.

The other minister was called Adam Martindale who was born at Prescot, Lancashire in 1623. By the time he was seven he loved to read all day long, the Bible and any other book that came to hand. He had several wonderful escapes too, through the Lord's good hand: he narrowly escaped drowning, and was once rescued from falling down a coalpit. After going to different schools and becoming a tutor himself, he returned home when he was eighteen, and then it was that he heard a minister preach, and he was pricked in his heart like those we read of in the Acts: the words he heard were 'like a sharp needle, drawing after a silken thread of comfort in due season'.

Soon he became the Master of the Free School at Over Whitley, and a good teacher he made too, although he was not quite twenty years old. Then the plague visited Cheshire, and so many ministers died that he consented to preach, starting off with Ephesians 2, verses 5 and 6, lovely verses

that you can look up yourselves. The next year 1646 he
became the minister at Gorton, Manchester and carried on
preaching where God led him until that same awful day, 24th
August 1662, when he was ejected just like John Machin.
But he still carried on preaching, in spite of much trouble,
until his death on 21st September 1686. His *Life* was
published afterward by the Cheetham Society. I am sure that
it would have done Mr. Herring good to know the Lord was
raising up these men to take his place in those needy parts.
God is like that: He knows all the needs, and He knows just
exactly how to supply them in His time and way.

Another minister in those parts, Henry Newcombe at
Gawsforth, Cheshire, used to get his books sent up from
London by his sister who lived there. But oh dear, they were
wrapped up with sugar at the other end of the parcel, and the
carter got the parcel wet – you can imagine how they arrived
at their destination, quite spoilt! The men often seemed to
handle parcels roughly, and his books would come in halves,
or spoilt, or were lost completely. But when his books
arrived, he looked after them and read them well.

He said as he got older, "At my first conversion, I thought
very few to be of my spirit, few right; and I taxed many old
ministers with formality. But now, bless God, I do
exceedingly honour and prefer them all, and count myself
least of all."

When he first started to preach, he was only twenty: at first
he put too much history in his sermons, so that when the
people came expecting to look the things up in their Bibles,
they were disappointed. But religion came to mean much to
him. And then he used his Bible more than most.

How different to the people at Congleton, Cheshire. By
1662 *their* church Bible was worn out, so they collected
money to buy a new one. But when they had enough, the
cruel sport of bear-baiting, which the Puritans had stopped,
was revived – so they bought a bear instead! It led to a local
saying, 'selling the Word of God to buy a bear.'

Mr. Ball
and the Children

MR. Ball was always looked upon by Christian people as a very contented man; the secret of the Lord was with him (Psa. 25). He used to say that one thought of Jesus, *reaching the heart,* was worth more than all the comfortable, happy, earthly things you could have, even if you had them all for a thousand years.

When the tyranny of the archbishop grew very hot, he and his friend, "the meek Mr. Langley," were chosen by some of the Puritans to go to London, to see if by a talk with some Members of Parliament some liberty might be granted to many godly preachers who were silenced at that time. The two good men came back in sorrow however; they had obtained nothing. They were not indeed surprised, and Mr. Ball felt as he had always felt that his work was not to rule, but to preach, teach, and write. He was writing a catechism for children that very year—1640—and might have finished and published it, but an illness came—his last—and in the autumn he died.

Mr. Ball had seven children—six boys and one girl. In the

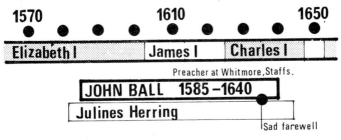

1570   1610   1650

Elizabeth I   James I   Charles I

Preacher at Whitmore, Staffs.

JOHN BALL 1585–1640

Julines Herring

Sad farewell

title "Mr. Ball and the Children," however, other children as well as his are intended, viz., Dr. Willet's eighteen, and Mr. Herring's thirteen for although the records of other days tell us chiefly about the fathers, it would be a pity to leave out anything that we can glean about the children. These fathers—and mothers—had the very same wishes and prayers for their children as so many of *your* parents have. They brought them up in the fear of God, and prayed that God would bless His Word to them and save their souls.

I have found a book of very old-fashioned hymns and poems, and one of them is by Dr. Willet. It is a very simple one for children:—

> "Jacob did see a ladder high
>   As he was laid asleep,
> The angels come and go thereby
>   Which do him safely keep.
>
> We learn hereby in every way
>   That God must be our Guide;
> Or else we soon may go astray
>   Our foot is apt to slide."

Dr. Willet thought it was quite a rest, after he had been writing his learned books, to sing hymns like that with the little ones. One of these 'little ones,' the eldest son sailed to America when he became a man. He went to New York; it was really 'new' in those days, and he became its first mayor. I do not know why he left England; it might not have been for the reason that the Pilgrim Fathers left it, viz., to gain freedom to worship God, but if he had the God of Jacob to be his God and his Guide, as the hymn said, he would be a blessed man and he would *be* a blessing, whatever his profession or his trade was in New York.

As to Mr. Herring's thirteen children, they all had to learn the whole of the book of Proverbs and repeat the verses to their mother. There are thirty-one chapters in Proverbs and they learnt them all. These children grew up to be great comforts to their parents. It was said of them: "The blossoms

and fruits of grace appeared in their lives."

And now for Mr. Ball's seven children. *Changes for the better!* Mr. Ball was a private chaplain to a squire Mr. Edward Mainwaring, and the neighbours used to come into 'the great parlour' in the Manor House at Whitmore in Staffordshire to hear him preach. Very many sound, able, silenced ministers were chaplains in private families, but the time came when Archbishop Laud, hunting the godly, said that no gentleman without a title, no mere esquire, might keep a chaplain. Mr. Ball preached in the village and kept a school, and so was Schoolmaster to his seven children as well as father.

But for the school he would have had no more than £20 a year. His house however had been given to him by Mr. Mainwaring, who also gave him a field and a cow, and so with "Sir, my father sent you this cheese"; and "Mam, my mother is sending you a goose," from the pupils, they got on so comfortably that Mr. Ball was continually full of thankfulness. He gave all the children an excellent education. The chief thing recorded about him and his children is this: when he asked a blessing at meals he always prayed for them, that they might be taught by God not to seek great things for themselves. "Life! life! eternal life!" was the chief thing, and Mr. Ball remembered Baruch in the forty-fifth chapter of Jeremiah to whom the Lord said: "And seekest thou great things for thyself? seek them not: for, behold, I will bring evil upon all flesh, saith the Lord: but thy life will I give unto thee for a prey in all places whither thou goest."

Lady Bromley of Sheriff Hales in Shropshire, often gave shelter to the persecuted ministers of Jesus Christ when they were hounded out of their livings. Mr. Ball, Mr. Nicolls, Mr. Pierson, Mr. Herring and others, all found a welcoming sanctuary under her roof. They preached nearby whenever they could, and when they were prevented, they kept days of fasting and humiliation at her house.

Though Mr. Ball was comparatively poor, having only twenty pounds a year, he was quite content saying, "I have *enough, enough, enough*." And the poor found he was always ready to help them. One friend who was tired of school-teaching, said he wished instead to enter the ministry; Mr. Ball replied, "You will find it far more difficult to teach men than boys!" And he knew what he was talking about, as I said, because after preaching on the Lord's Day, he taught at school in the village all week for his further support!

Another friend once told him what a danger he had been in, having fallen from his horse – he had never experienced so great a deliverance before! "Yes, you have," said Mr. Ball, "a hundred times – even as often as you have ridden and *not* fallen."

To people with unruly tempers, he used to say, "Put judgment into office. The affections are bad guides, but good followers. Look well to your hearts. Passion is the effect of pride. You ride an unruly horse, and therefore you stand in need of a strong bit and bridle."

Judgments

THE well-known public school at Oundle in Northamptonshire had been established forty years when about 1590 Hugh Clark, a young man not thirty years old, became a minister there. Whether or not the whole generation had been instructed in the New Learning, they had not been brought up on Reformation doctrine and practice, but still followed many old Romish customs. Mr. Clark found them very much addicted to Morris dancing on the Lord's day and tried to teach them to keep the day holy. They opposed him strongly, "but," as Samuel Clark, his son and biographer, puts it, "the judgment of God found them out for their wickedness." On a Lord's day the leader fell down dead in the middle of the dance; the others were startled, but shook off their fears and went on with the dance.

The Sabbath morning following Mr. Clark preached against the sin of Sabbath-breaking, and quoted Jeremiah 17. 27: "If thou wilt not hearken unto Me to hallow the Sabbath day . . . then will I kindle a fire in the gates and it shall devour the palaces of Jerusalem, and it shall not be

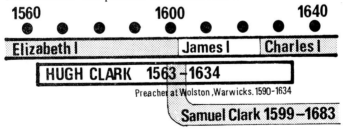

1560   1600   1640

Elizabeth I   James I   Charles I

HUGH CLARK 1563-1634

Preacher at Wolston, Warwicks. 1590-1634

Samuel Clark 1599-1683

OLD OUNDLE

quenched." And yet in the evening the people returned to the sports and dancing on the green. Their captain was the town blacksmith. His smithy was a long low thatched building next to his thatched house.

On Monday two ploughmen came to have their ploughshares sharpened. As the smith beat the red-hot iron on the anvil a spark flew into the thatch. They all saw it and stood gazing, as if quite powerless to put it out, although for some minutes the burnt spot of thatch might easily have been pulled down with the fingers. Presently the whole place was on fire. The men ran out and the shop, house, and all the blacksmith's perishable goods were consumed. Yet although this was a literal fulfilment of the passage their minister had quoted to them, they still went on with their Sunday games.

Very soon after that, when they had been drinking to excess and dancing on the Lord's day evening and had gone home, they imagined that they heard a great noise of rattling chains up and down the street, and that there was a strong smell of fire and brimstone. Many of them believed, they

OLD OUNDLE

said, that the devil had come to carry them to hell. They were terrified, and after that some began to attend to the preaching. A reformation began and before Hugh Clark left Oundle he was happy in seeing sixteen of these people "sitting at the feet of Jesus, clothed and in their right mind." Some who continued to flout his ministry to the end were strangely reduced to complete beggary.

Samuel Clark has other stories to tell of his father's struggles in these rough times. One of the Oundle men came with a concealed dagger to "have talk with him," but his minister's words drew from him a trembling confession of his wicked intent to stab him. He went away forgiven. This son Samuel grew up and became a minister himself, and many of the stories in this book were of ministers who belonged to his father's generation: no doubt they told them over the family meal-table, and he must have known a good number of them personally.

When he was old enough, he went up to Emmanuel College, Cambridge, and there his tutor was none other than Thomas Hooker who was so comforted and instructed by Simeon Ash (page 33). After college, Samuel went to be minister at Thornton-in-the-Moors, and his experience was

OUNDLE CHURCH

SAMUEL CLARK

much deepened: he says, "I was never acquainted with more understanding Christians in my life, though the best wore russet coats and followed husbandry – how we Christians loved each other!" He afterward moved for a while to Shotwick, Cheshire, and after that became the distinguished minister at one of the London churches, St. Benet Fink.

Now he felt what a good thing it would be to have all those facts down on paper about the ministers he had known, and so he started writing his books and getting pictures of the men where he could: most people who have since written on the lives of these old ministers have gone back to Samuel Clark's books. When we found a portrait of Samuel we thought you would like to see it.

But now we must return to his father Hugh, who was still a young man when he moved from Oundle to be minister at Wolston in Warwickshire. Once he was waylaid in a wood when he was going home from Coventry alone, and with nothing but a walking-stick in his hand. A man whose conscience had been galled by the preaching, rode up and fell into conversation with him. The same trembling confession of his resolve to murder him was the result. But that man went back to his wicked ways, and God's judgments found him out at last, for though he had a very good living he fell into misery and want and died in Warwick Gaol for debt.

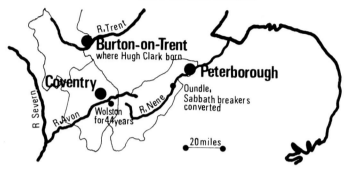

One bishop who had tried to hinder Mr. Clark from going to Wolston went one day to hear him preach, with the purpose of finding some fault, so that he could get rid of him at last. Mr. Clark preached as earnestly as usual, and the bishop grew more and more vexed, moving from pew to pew as if he were sitting on thorns; someone fetched him a cushion to make him more comfortable, but of course it was his mind, not his body, that was displeased. When Mr. Clark had finished, the bishop stood up before everyone and said, 'This is indeed a hot fellow, but I will cool him.' Mr. Clark simply said, 'If you will show me where I did not faithfully deliver God's truth, I will put it right before everyone at once;' but the bishop said no more and stormed out. First the bishop suspended him from preaching, so Mr. Clark then 'expounded'; then he suspended him from expounding, so Mr. Clark catechized with question and answer. And when the bishop suspended him from catechizing, Mr. Clark got a godly man at the usual time of sermon to read a chapter to the people; at the end of every verse the man asked Mr. Clark the meaning of it, and what instructions flowed from it! This made the bishop, when he heard of it, so cross that he excommunicated poor Mr. Clark, and even brought it to pass that Hugh Clark was put in Warwick Gaol for a time. He had prayed in a public prayer that God would forgive the Queen her sins, upon which the bishop charged him with treason and kept him in prison till the Assizes. There was in the court a man whose name figures in Shakespeare's life—Sir Thomas Lucy of Charlecote, with whom the poet is said to have got into trouble for poaching in his park. Mr. Clark however got *out* of trouble through Sir Thomas; he "stood up and publicly told the judge that before Master Clark should have any wrong, he would kneel before the Queen herself for him;" and so he was acquitted.

I am very glad to say that after this, the archbishop heard about it all, and he called both the bishop and Mr. Clark before him, and listened fully to what they both had to say – it is right to listen to both sides, and not make up our minds beforehand. After he had heard them, he told the bishop to go to Mr. Clark's church once more, and on the sabbath day before the whole congregation to make a public acknowledgement of the wrong he had done to Mr. Clark; and all this the bishop did. And what is best of all, from that time the bishop and Mr. Clark became the firmest of friends till the end of their lives.

Mr. Clark had a chapel of ease some distance away from the church at Wolston, and he preached twice every sabbath here too, so he was kept very busy; and this went on for nearly 44 years. He had seven children, and he lived to see the work of grace begun in every one of them.

Writers of fiction who have disliked Puritanism in all its forms have loved to depict the stern Puritan calling down judgment and washing his feet in the blood of the wicked. But it was no new thing to notice judgments. Good men had always observed them; they spoke with a loud voice saying, "Except ye repent, ye shall all likewise perish." Wicked men had noticed them, but repented not. To see judgments superstitiously where they were not, was much more a feature of Popery than of Protestantism. Samuel Clark is one of the Puritan writers who perhaps more than others does not hesitate to say, "The judgment of God found them out." He has a whole chapter in his *Martyrology* on The Judgments of God upon Persecutors, but these incidents in his father's life are of his recounting, and the novelists' theory of the Puritan gloating over calamities or calling judgment down, is not here; Hugh Clark rejoiced in the repentance of his poor people, and forgave the men who would have murdered him. He knew that 'repentance toward God, and faith in Jesus Christ' is a *change for the better* in the heart of any man, and the power of God the Holy Spirit can accomplish it in us today.

You will remember perhaps that in Elizabeth's days the godly preachers wanted to spread the knowledge of the scriptures far and wide, and wonderful too was the fact that so many people wanted to listen to them at every opportunity. This is how the 'Prophesyings' began, when people would flock together to listen. At many different centres up and down the land they arranged these meetings, and a description of one they held at Norwich has come down to us; this is what happened.

The Prophesy was held every Monday morning at 9 o'clock till eleven; there was a list of local ministers that were invited to take part if they wished, and the text for the day had already been given. So there the ministers sit side by side, waiting for the meeting to begin; the chairman was the speaker of the week before; and when he was ready he would take off his hat, and the first speaker then preached a sermon for about three-quarters of an hour; then the other ministers could add anything to what had been said – they went along the line, and if a minister had nothing to add, he put on his hat, and then it was the turn of the next to him, and so on. After the two hours were up, the chairman concluded with prayer.

They were to speak in English, so that everyone who gathered could understand; they were not to repeat themselves, and to avoid controversy, so that all the people could learn just what the scriptures taught. No one was to speak 'hastily, rashly, disorderly, but soberly and reverendly as in the presence of God.'

After the Prophesy was ended, all the ministers met on their own, and made helpful comments on the first speaker's sermon, on how he had handled the text, and on his way of 'delivery', so that by these kindly corrections they all helped one another to be better and more able ministers of the gospel. Then at the end, the one who had been the first speaker, and who would be the chairman on the following Monday morning, suggested the text to be considered on that occasion.

These were the Prophesyings then that the enemies of the gospel wanted brought to an end; and you will remember that when they had influenced the Queen to give the Order to stop them, Archbishop Grindal wept for grief and wrote the Queen that touching appeal against her decision*. No wonder, for he could see what good the meetings were doing for the ordinary people of the land he loved.

And what was happening back at Oundle all this time? Well, even before Mr. Hugh Clark went there, there had been 'Prophesyings' held there in 1574-6, just the same as the one you read of on page 9. I thought you would like to hear what they did at such meetings.

Mr. Hugh Clark had gone to Oundle after this, and as you have read, he began to see the Lord blessing his ministry before he left. But as the years went by, the Lord did not leave off His work at Oundle. In Oliver Cromwell's days, a Mr. Richard Resbury was made the 'lecturer' at Oundle to help teach the people, and later he was made the vicar – though I like the way he called himself simply 'Minister of the Gospel at Oundle.' He was an Independent and a Calvinist, who wrote against Arminianism, which is the teaching that man by his own free-will can turn to God when he likes. A book in which Mr. Resbury taught what was right, printed in 1651, is still in the Library of Oundle School. Now Oundle School was looked after by the Grocers' Company of London, where they had their own minister: so every so often some Grocers would come down to the School to see that everything was being done properly by the Schoolmaster and the managers.

So it happened that one Monday morning in June 1650 ten of them set off from London, including their minister from St Stephens church, Walbrook, Thomas Watson, in two coaches: they arrived in Oundle 80 miles away on Tuesday evening. The London visitors examined everything on Wednesday – there were sixty-seven boys at the School: the

* Changes For the Better, volume 1, pages 85-93.

chained books were found in position: the schoolmaster's house was clean, handsome and well-furnished with books – and so the London Visitors said the boys could have half-a-day off! On Thursday they all went to the church to hear Mr. Resbury preach morning and afternoon; and on Friday they started off once more from Oundle, reaching London on Saturday night.

I expect Mr. Resbury the Oundle minister and Mr. Watson the minister from London had a few friendly talks, and told each other about what the Lord had done for them. Thomas Watson was a good man, whose books are still published today: perhaps he told Mr. Resbury of the time the Bishop came to hear him in London: the Bishop was pleased with the sermon and especially with the prayer after it, so he followed Mr. Watson home and asked him for a copy of his prayer (the Bishop used prayers already written out for him). 'Alas,' Mr. Watson had said, 'that is what I cannot give you, for I do not write out my prayers; I utter the words as God enables me, out of the abundance of my heart and affections.' And the disappointed Bishop, good man, had to go away empty, marvelling that any man could pray like that! Well, Mr. Watson's prayers were *real*.

In the Month of May

MR Isaac Ambrose was very ill indeed in the early spring of 1653; he was the minister at Preston in Lancashire, a busy town, with such a lot to attend to among all his people; and at last when he began to feel as if he might get better of the 'sore sickness' he went away for a month to a little hide-away place in the woods near Garstang. And there in the springtime, all alone except for the singing of the birds and the wind in the trees, he felt the presence of His Lord and Saviour very specially. One scripture after another kept shining into his mind, and made it a real springtime in his heart; he felt Jesus so precious, and he knew that was what a soul really needed. That time in the woods did him so much

PRESTON CHURCH

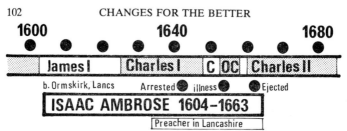

good that he started writing a book about his beloved Lord, and he called it *Looking Unto Jesus*; and he decided every year he would come again at the same time, and spend the month of May in his solitary retreat.

Some kind friends took me to see where he used to go; his retreat was in Woodacre Great Wood, about a third of a mile north of Woodacre Hall, but of course things have altered. In the 1800s they made a railway line, and the Barnacre cutting went within yards of the spot; then in this century they made the M6, which went within six yards on the *other* side, parallel to the railway line; so that where he used to stay in solitude is now a narrow little strip of land in between the busy bustle of men. But just over the hill, one is back again, away from the busy traffic, in the lovely woods, and in the stillness with just the sound of a rippling stream over the rocks, it is easy to imagine once more the good minister Isaac Ambrose walking, thinking, praying, communing with his Lord. He spent a lot of time too in the woods on the edge of the Darwen. Let me tell you his story.

He was born on 29th May 1604, so he was only in his late forties when he was so poorly; he was the youngest of three boys and three girls and his birthplace was Ormskirk; a good man started a Free Grammar School there in 1612, and I should think eight-year-old Isaac was among the first pupils, for he went on to Brazenose College, Oxford, and gained a B.A. degree, and then after that to Magdalen College, Cambridge, where he graduated M.A.

When he was only 23 he became vicar at Castleton in Derbyshire, and he was pastor there about four years, serving his people in his first love to the Lord, who blessed him there. Many years after, when Castleton was mentioned, tears came to his eyes, and he said, "It was my sin, and is my

CASTLETON CHURCH

sorrow, that I left that place when the Lord was blessing my ministry in it." But the Lord was forging other links in the chain of His providence. For he had paid a visit to Woburn, and was befriended by William, the Earl of Bedford. He saw how they enjoyed morning and evening prayer in that household; his heart was cheered as he talked with the Christian servants there. And evidently *he* cheered the Earl's heart, for he started to support Mr. Ambrose with welcome aid; and carried on doing so year after year for over twenty years – for it is one thing to start, quite another to keep carrying on. But it did not stop there. The Earl soon took care to have Mr Ambrose appointed one of the four King's Preachers for Lancashire; and so he came to settle in his native county, making Garstang his base for his preaching journeys, early in 1634; and I think that marrying his young lady, Judith, all helped him to make a happy home; and inside a year a little baby girl Rachel came to share their home too! Later there came two little boys, first Augustine, and later Richard. How quickly those six or seven years passed; he grew to love the Garstang people, and they loved him; but all the while he was not their vicar, but the King's

ISAAC AMBROSE

Preacher for that part of Lancashire. I wonder how many
nights he had to stop away from home, away from his little
family.

But the wheels of the Lord's providence were slowly
revolving to accomplish His will. Through his friendship with
the Houghton family, Lady Margaret Houghton presented
him to be vicar of Preston; and there he and his little family
moved; and as he still kept his office as 'King's Preacher' he
would be busy.

About this time, in 1641, he began to keep his Diary, a
'Register of God's dealings towards him, and of his dealings
towards God'; shall we peep over his shoulder to see what he
is writing? 'May 20th. This day in the evening the Lord in His
mercy poured into my soul the ravishing joy of His blessed
Spirit. O how sweet was the Lord unto me! I never felt such a
lovely taste of heaven before.' But it was not to be all honey
for Isaac! Only the next year the Civil Wars were beginning
to rage, and spies on both sides were never far away,

sometimes making trouble out of nothing. And poor Isaac found himself taken to prison by the Commissioners of Array. His flock – what would they do? his family – how would they fare? But the Lord had it all mapped out. Over in York the other side of the Pennines, were three good folk – Stephen Watson, a grocer who was Lord Mayor of York a few years later in 1646; John Geldart, a merchant there, who had his turn as Lord Mayor in 1645; and Thomas Nisbet, another merchant. And these three worthy friends helped his wife with the three needy children, and one or other of them spent a happy holiday for a time with one of these 'uncles' – and I expect the kind 'aunts' too.

It seems that part of his captivity – for he was imprisoned twice at different times – was spent at London, where the Lord gave him things that made his heart prosper, over against the adverse things. For "God also hath set the one over against the other, to the end that man should find nothing after him" (Ecclesiastes 7. 14). For one thing, he enjoyed meeting Simeon Ash – do you remember? – whom the Lord gave a new heart while listening to Julines Herring at Calke (page 33). And for another, he became acquainted with Lady Mary Vere, and was able to be with her at an observance of the Lord's Supper; and when they parted, she left a nice gift in his hand to help him along in his difficulties.

Isaac was not kept in prison long, and another friend, William Farrington of Worden, helped him all the while he was in prison; and on obtaining his release brought him home

Garstang — His first base when King's preacher for Lancashire. Later Vicar there.

R. Ribble

Preston
died here

LANCASHIRE

Ormskirk
where Ambrose born

YORKSHIRE

20 miles

Vicar for 4yrs
Castleton

to his wife and children loaded with kindnesses. Isaac never forgot it; for he knew from sad experience what it was to be in prison; so you can imagine that when, only a few years after, it was the turn of his friend William to be imprisoned, Isaac was busy straight away trying to get his friend released, writing a certificate to show his innocence of any crime. And after ten months had gone by, the Parliamentary soldiers let his friend William go on payment of a fine.

Isaac started writing good books, so that the gospel might reach even further; and as there was still no printing-press in the whole of Lancashire, they had to be printed in London; so what with preaching, visiting, writing, proof-reading, his time was taken up – he was well described as a 'painful minister', that is, a painstaking one. Small wonder that some-one had to draw attention to the fact that in December 1651 the parish registers were not being kept quite up-to-date by the pastor.

Then came his illness, and his convalescence in the woods near Garstang. Do you know, the good folk at Garstang had never forgotten him, and never forgotten his loving faithful ministry. Back in 1640 they had appealed to have him as their vicar; and now fourteen years later they were still as anxious as ever – doesn't it remind you of how long Jacob was prepared to work for his Rachel? so they kept on asking for their Mr. Ambrose, for he was to many their 'spiritual father' and they knew so well his 'tender care'. Their touching letter of appeal had twenty-eight signatures, and off it went to the Committee of Triers at the Savoy in London. Now just as the Committee were considering it – and how did *they* know anyone all that way away? – the Master of the Savoy came in at that instant, heard Garstang mentioned, and as he knew Ambrose, he remembered him as 'the most fit person for that people,' and it 'was set home upon his heart'. So he obtained the living for him, and sent to Mr. Ambrose to tell him. Although he had often thought how much he would like to go to Garstang again, now the time came, and he found the love of *both* peoples pulling him in two. The Preston people wept as if it was his funeral; they could not let him go! He lived on at Preston – the old vicarage where he lived was

ST. HELENS, CHURCHTOWN, GARSTANG
A 12th century church known as the Cathedral of Fylde

in Lancaster Road, near where the Congregational chapel is now – quite some time after his appointment to Garstang, but his health was not what it was; he needed a smaller place than the busy town, and at last he moved, saying, "I feel my stars darken and the clouds to return after rain . . . my work before me is less with man and more with God." The Garstang church was the old one at Churchtown, with its striking vestry, texts painted all round the top of the arches in the nave, and the very pulpit where he preached still there today.

Mr. Ambrose was called to go back once to Preston to fulfil a very sad duty – to conduct the funeral of his friend Lady Margaret Houghton, on 4th January 1657. We do not know why, but the funeral was arranged to take place at night, and only with great difficulty could the cortege pass through the streets, the people were so packed. They could hardly enter the church door, and after the body was laid to rest, poor Mr. Ambrose just could not make his voice heard, although he strained his voice to the highest pitch. Some of the folk were standing on the seats; so at length, because so many just failed to hear, he had the sermon printed so that they *could* have it: it was called *Redeeming The Time*, from Ephesians 5. 16.

For several more years he wrote and laboured earnestly and lovingly; but then that sad Bartholomew's Day in August

1662 overtook him, and with so many more hundreds of good ministers all over England, he was ejected from his place. He went back to Preston to live in retirement in the Church Weind, now Tithebarn Street. Just over a year later, in the January, some of his Garstang people came to visit their old pastor. He was so glad to see them, and told them he had now finished writing all the books he intended, having sent away only the night before his *Discourse Concerning Angels* to the press. He went to see them off on their horses, and returning into his house, went to his room. The others thought, 'He *is* a long while', and so opening the door into his room, they found him just dying. Death, like a clock, gave him little warning before it struck. He was buried at Preston, and his dear widow Judith went to live with their daughter Rachel, now married, with children of her own, at Bolton. Her mother lived four more years before she too was taken; and only the next year, Rachel herself died, aged only 34, leaving twelve-year-old Benjamin and ten-year-old Hannah. I wonder if we shall meet them one day.

So Isaac Ambrose lived and died; he was a most peaceful man, though he lived in upsetting times. He saw fathers siding against their children, and brothers fighting under different banners, but he never flinched from duty, was never absent from his post, and his spirit was so loving and gentle that no bitterness escaped his lips.

But he left his writings for those who are left. He wrote of *Prima*, the *first* things God's children are taught in conversion; *Media*, the *middle* things they need to know in the Christian pilgrimage here below; and *Ultima*, the *last* things we must come to – death, the resurrection, the judgment, heaven or hell. But the book he decided to write after he had been so ill was his most famous one; it is called *Looking Unto Jesus* (Hebrews 12. 2). It has been printed many times in English and has been translated into Dutch; and all through the years, through God's blessing, it has done many people good. He cast his bread upon the waters, and it is found after many days.

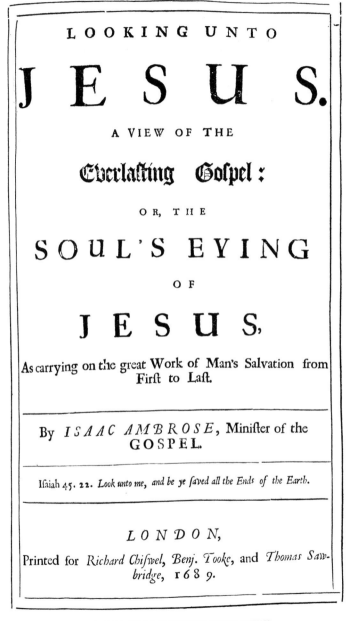

LOOKING UNTO

JESUS.

A VIEW OF THE

Everlasting Gospel:

OR, THE

SOUL'S EYING

OF

JESUS,

As carrying on the great Work of Man's Salvation from First to Last.

By *ISAAC AMBROSE*, Minister of the GOSPEL.

Isaiah 45. 22. *Look unto me, and be ye saved all the Ends of the Earth.*

LONDON,

Printed for *Richard Chiswel, Benj. Tooke,* and *Thomas Sawbridge,* 1689.

TITLE PAGE OF '*LOOKING UNTO JESUS*'

So Isaac had a lot to do with books in his lifetime, and as I explained there was no printing-press in Lancashire yet: they were mostly printed in London in those days, and had to be brought by the carriers.

Only a few years ago there lived an ageing mother over in Holland, where Ambrose's works, translated into Dutch are still occasionally to be found. Mother was very troubled in her soul: her sins lay heavy on her conscience, and she knew of no-one to whom she could talk about such things. Alone in the house at Franeker, how she longed to know one who knew what it was to feel as she did. But none of those she knew in the neighbourhood thought anything of such things.

In her sadness, Mother picked up one of the well-worn books of the home, one by Isaac Ambrose. As she read, she found what did her heart good; the Holy Spirit so used it that she knew she was hearing God speaking to her through the words as she sat there on her own; sacred moments — but who is that knocking hard on the door? Only the baker, surely; what an unwelcome interruption! Going to the door, true, there was the baker, but looking the house up and down — what did that mean? "Do you know," he said, "I used to live here 30 years ago. I should like to see round the old haunts." "Come in then," said Mother, "I'm sure you're very welcome." At length he spotted Ambrose, still lying open — "You have a good book there," he said earnestly. And then the baker began to speak of things he knew and felt in his heart, that described just what Mother herself was feeling! How eagerly she listened, for she knew now the Lord had seen her, heard her, sent her a man who understood what a living exercised soul feels within. It was the Lord's doing, and it was marvellous in her eyes! Two of them, *looking unto Jesus*.

The Good Lord Wharton

PHILIP, the fourth Lord Wharton, was born on 18th April 1613; he was a fine-looking lad, who grew up to be very handsome. He was not without sad times though, for his father died when Philip was only nine. This meant that when his grandfather died, he could expect to come into the title and an inheritance of £8000 a year, and in those days that meant a vast sum of money.

When he was twelve, his grandfather died; and Philip grew up in society, admired for his fine figure, spending his leisure in dancing and other amusements. When he was about twenty he married, and they had a little daughter who eventually grew up and married Robert Bertie, Lord Willoughby d'Eresby — but that is another story. Sad to say, his wife died; and it was some years after that he married again. His second wife was Jane Goodwyn of Winchendon near Aylesbury, Bucks. I think the Lord was using these links to make Lord Wharton think about the things that matter most, about God, his soul, the Saviour and the Word of God. By this marriage there were three sons and four daughters born; but again he lost his dear wife, just a few days after his 45th birthday. Three years later he married again, and had another little boy.

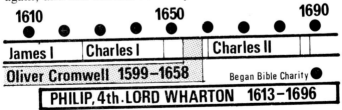

But we must follow Lord Wharton himself now through his life in those stirring days. For after he was brought to think seriously about things, and was taught by the Lord, he found himself on the side of Parliament when King Charles the First wanted to do just as he liked in taxing his people. At last the two sides started to fight, and Lord Wharton was on the Parliament side. He took part in the fight at Edgehill on 23rd October 1642, when he was 29, although a good many on their side ran away; though he himself stayed in the battle all

PHILIP, LORD WHARTON

night, he did not feel as well qualified as others for warfare, and felt he could do more good in Parliament.

When things were more settled, he was a lay member of the Westminster Assembly of Divines, which tried to get a proper settled basis for the Church of England according to the scriptures. But not everyone agreed; some wanted presbyterianism, with a national body of elders in control over the churches, but others including Lord Wharton wanted to see each local church able to act on its own according to what it felt was right from the Bible. Those who wanted such toleration for 'gathered churches' were in the minority, and Lord Wharton suggested in the House of Lords that the Assembly be dissolved, for he could see the dangers of a rigid uniform system such as most wanted. However, Cromwell came to power, and he favoured the toleration of all good and godly men, so that they could each act according to his conscience by the scripture — he felt if a man was a spiritual minister taught of God, he should be allowed to preach; so in his days you could find some Baptists who were ministers in the Church of England. And Lord Wharton was one who helped in making sure that only good godly ministers were appointed to the various churches; it happened that on his own estates he often had the right to choose the minister, and so he was able to give the places to good Puritan ministers, 'able ministers of the New Testament.' He and Oliver Cromwell were good friends; Oliver sometimes stayed at his house, and afterward, when he wrote to Lord Wharton, he added "My love to the dear little lady (Jane Goodwyn)...The Lord bless you both." Though Lord Wharton became uneasy, and disapproved of the execution of the king, the friendship was not broken. But Lord Wharton went to live now mostly in the country, and withdrew from parliamentary life.

Well, how *did* Lord Wharton know whether a man was suitable to be a minister for one of his churches? We hear of one man who came to obtain one. Lord Wharton said, "Sir, it is my custom to give such a place on three conditions: first, the minister must pray in my family — I don't mean *read* prayers, for any of my servants who can read can do that;

second, he must preach in my family so that I may have a taste of his talent that way; and then third, he is to go to the parish, and if the people approve of him the living is his."

He lived mostly at Upper Winchendon, where most of his children were born; but when Lady Jane died in 1658 he removed to the old Manor House of Wooburn, sixteen miles away. This house used to be a palace of the Bishops of Lincoln, and next to its chapel was a prison where some of the early Protestant martyrs were kept; it was called Little Ease because it was not big enough for a prisoner either to stand upright or to lie at length; in it Thomas Chase of Amersham was privately strangled for heresy in 1506, and Thomas Harden of Chesham and others were kept there before being burnt at the stake in 1532. So now the old Manor House was to echo to the glad truths for which those sufferers had witnessed — it was indeed *a change for the better*. He spent a lot of money on improving the building, which a century later was demolished.

At length the monarchy was restored, and Lord Wharton trusted the word of King Charles II that there would be toleration in the national church if he came back. Lord Wharton was among the cavalcade formed to welcome the King at Greenwich, his black clothing sparkling with diamond buttons, and his horse furniture gleaming. But he had enemies who hated him for his religion, and who plotted his death by getting his name on the list of those excepted by the King from the general pardon. His daughter Lady

Willoughby was crossing the ferry at Lambeth, and overheard a gentleman mention her father's name and the plan to get rid of him; when she got home, she mentioned it to her husband, who had been a Cavalier, and he was able to speak with the King and get Lord Wharton's name crossed off; what a wonderful example of the Lord's good providence.

Soon the promise the King had made for religious toleration was broken; and the Act of Uniformity was designed in 1662 to get rid of as many conscientous puritan ministers as possible from being the ministers in the national church. When the Act came before the Lords, he was on the committee to consider it, but being in a small minority he could not prevent it being passed. He opposed the passing of the Conventicle Act in 1664 and the Five Mile Act in 1665, which were also designed to stamp out the Nonconformists once and for all. Lord Wharton did his utmost to lessen the damage these Acts caused.

Next door to his London home in St. Giles, Dr. Manton (ejected from St. Pauls, Covent Garden) had a meeting room—or should I say rooms, for often there were three rooms full of worshipping folk gathered to hear the persecuted ministers; Lord Wharton was often there as a hearer. Once their illegal meeting was broken into; they pretended not to know Lord Wharton; and after the minister and others were fined £60, Lord Wharton paid it all. Dr. Manton was welcome to the use of his house. All over the country, in London, in Buckinghamshire, in his houses on his northern estates, Lord Wharton tried to find some way of making these ejected ministers useful where they could still preach. He corresponded with Joseph Alleine in Somerset as to how Wales could be reached with the gospel.

The mansion at Wooburn, near the wooded hills, with its own row of stately poplars, was often the gathering-place for folk from the countryside around to come and listen to the gospel being preached in the chapel there; after the morning service they were invited to the house for refreshment before the afternoon service.

Up in the north, he made one ejected minister steward of

his lead mines; and many more were befriended in Yorkshire and Westmorland.

Things did not get better. Lord Wharton opposed the new Conventicle Act in 1670, and was always striving to uphold the Protestant cause. He was even sent to the Tower for five months; and when James II came to the throne, and the Nonconformists were plotted against worse than ever, he felt it safest to go abroad; and for a year travelled in Holland, Germany, France and Flanders. He had John Howe for his chaplain.

At length the tide turned, and Lord Wharton was among the first to welcome the landing of the Prince of Orange, was sworn Privy Councillor, and did his part in passing the Act of Toleration, which allowed the persecuted people of God to worship more freely again. William III visited Wooburn in 1689, which was a great honour. Lord Wharton had Wooburn licensed as a meeting-place for Protestant Dissenters; he made an annual allowance to many Non-conformist ministers in various places; and he maintained poor scholars at the schools and academies which Noncon-formist ministers had commenced. He built a meeting-house in Swaledale near the lead mines; another in Ravenstonedale for his tenants and other dalesmen. The minister there, after the Ejection, once met some other ministers who had conformed, and who pointed out that he had a threadbare coat: he replied, "If my coat is bare, it is not *turned*."

Lord Wharton was now well on in his seventies; his four sons often attended him, and a grand sight it was; one of them invented the first effective fire-engine, and once fished up out of St. George's Channel fourteen large cast-iron cannon, relics of the Spanish Armada.

But now troubles came nearer home; his youngest son was killed in a duel; in 1689 another died in Ireland, and the same year his daughter and her husband died within three weeks of each other, and the husband of another daughter was assassinated at Edinburgh. And not long after, his wife Lady Jane, who had been his companion and helpmeet over thirty years, was taken from him. But all these losses made him only more intent to 'serve the will of God in his own generation before he fell on sleep.'

So it came to pass in 1690, when he was 77, he began his Bible charity! He could see that through all the national turmoils, so many had lost sight of the Bible, family prayer was left off, and indifference prevailed. So he arranged that ministers he knew, especially Protestant Dissenters, who should, *first,* choose poor children where they lived, and give them a Bible and the Assembly's Catechism; *second*, a year later, if those children were learning to read well, and could repeat seven specified psalms from memory, the best in every ten was to be rewarded with two other useful books; *thirdly*, the parents were to be given a shilling to encourage them to go on teaching their children; and *fourthly*, ten annual sermons on the Bible were to be preached in various places in turn and extempore prayers offered before and after them (extempore, means, thought at the time, not read from a book). Those who examined the children to see whether they knew their psalms properly were to be given half-a-crown. One of the reward books was Joseph Alleine's *Sure Guide to Heaven.*

To make sure that there would continue to be enough money to do all this after he was gone, Lord Wharton made a Trust, and left his lands at Synethwaite, Bilton, Walton & Bickerton in Yorkshire with all the rents and profits, to provide the income; so that they became known as The Bible Lands. All the Trustees were Nonconformists or Protestant Dissenters.

This is how it worked out. Each year 1050 Bibles were provided, bound up with the singing Psalms, of the English translation published by authority (that is, our Authorised Version), leather-bound, with strong brass clasps, embossed on the cover with the words 'By the will of Philip, Lord Wharton' and the year; and on the flyleaf the psalms the child had learnt—the 1st, 15th, 25th, 37th, 101st, 113th, 145th. The Bibles were sent out to the different places in October each year, and given out to the children on the second or third Tuesday in October; and at the same time the Bible sermon was to be preached.

This is where the Bibles went to:

YORKSHIRE

The city of York	100	Wakefield	30	Thirsk	10
Doncaster	20	Sheffield	50	Tadcaster	10
Pontefract	30	Richmond	40	Wetherby	10
Leeds	80	Northallerton	10	Knaresborough	10
Halifax	40	Bedale	10	Healaugh &	
Bradford	40	Boroughbridge	10	Catterton	30
Hartforth	10	The 3 Swaledale		Aske & Easby	10
		manors	60		

WESTMORLAND

Appleby	20	Kirkby Stephen	40
Kendal	20	Ravenstonedale	30
Langdale, Teeby, Bresherdale and		Shap, Reagill, Sleagill,	
Preston Patrick	30	Bampton, Carshullen and	
		Long Marton	50

CUMBERLAND

Carlisle	20	Caldbeck	16
Penrith	10	Croglin	4
Cockermouth	30	Dean, Whinfell, Broughton	
		and Birkby	20

BUCKINGHAMSHIRE

Winslow	10	Chesham	10
Aylesbury	20	Chipping Wycombe	10
Wendover	10	Great Marlow	10
Amersham	10	Beaconsfield	10
Wooburn	10	Winchendon & Waddesdon	10

If there were not enough children to take them all, then the Trustees were allowed to distribute them elsewhere. And if there was any surplus income, more Bibles could be given out. It *did* make a lot of work, although packing them up in tens instead of singles helped out a lot. One minister wrote in his diary in 1701, 'Occupied in disposing of Lord Wharton's Bibles procured for the poor children, orphans and servants, who hearing that they were come, came in great crowds, so that I was almost suffocated with the heat.' And again in 1705, 'I sometimes catechized above 50 children on the Lord's Day night, and afterwards heard two sets of them sing the appointed Psalms, that I have been fatigued and almost stifled, but revived to see the zeal of so many, some of whom

WOOBURN CHURCH

came many miles.' After he had seen the Trust working over 30 years, this minister described how when it was first established many young men and women of sixteen and seventeen came who knew no more than the Lord's Prayer, whereas after that time it was mostly children of six or seven, who now could repeat the Commandments, Creed, Catechisms and the Psalms, and many other people's children had been taught to read in hope of getting Bibles. It brought about a *change for the better.*

If you read over the psalms they had to learn, you will see what Lord Wharton felt himself. Incidentally, the 25th psalm is the first of the Alphabetical psalms in which the first letter of each verse in the Hebrew corresponds in more or less exact order with the alphabet. Psalm 37 has been described as 'Medicine against murmuring.' Psalm 113 is the first of the Hallelujah or Passover Psalms.

At length good Lord Wharton was taken to his rest; he died on 4th February 1696 aged 82, and was buried at Wooburn Church where there is a large monument of grey marble erected to his memory. He was truly 'taken away from the evil to come'. His sons had been brought up in the

Reformed faith, but the father could not give them grace; so although they always tried to maintain the Protestant cause, they really had no heart for their father's godliness. The good Lord Wharton's grandson, who inherited the title, was sent by his guardians to Geneva, to be brought up a Protestant, with a Huguenot for his tutor; but the lad deserted him, became later president of a freethinker's club, gambled all his fortune away, turned a Roman Catholic, was outlawed for treason and went to Spain; taken ill while riding through a small village, he was nursed by some monks and after a week buried in the monastery aged only 32. So that all that was left of the Wharton estates was the Bible Lands which he had been unable to touch.

The Bible charity continued down the years, and did untold good. Gradually it came into Church of England hands; and in 1871 the Bible Lands were sold, the income still to be used for the Bibles. In late years however the Trustees have altered things, so that it is no longer the faithful Authorised Version which is given out, as the founder intended; and this has led the Trinitarian Bible Society to provide Bibles in much the same way as good Lord Wharton purposed. I trust you may come to love the Psalms that he did, and possess the true living loving saving grace of God in your heart through the knowledge of the Lord and Saviour Jesus Christ.

A Burning and
a Shining Light

WHEN Joseph Alleine was twelve, all the family moved
away from Devizes in Wiltshire where they lived, because
the plague had reached the town, and many, many people
were dying. His father was a weaver, and I should rather
think he was descended from those French Christians that we
call Huguenots because Moses-like they had to leave their
native land for the reproach of Christ. The family now settled
at Poulshot, where the good minister taught the boys there –
some boarded at the Rectory; Joseph joined them, and
learnt so well that he got a place at Oxford just a few years
later. Now I must tell you what made Joseph want to get on
so.

The eldest boy in their family had already felt the call to be
a minister, and Joseph while still a boy had felt deeply what a
serious thing this was. The Lord began to work in his mind,
and made him think about his soul and God, eternity and the
Saviour, death and life. And a little while later when he was
only eleven, Joseph's eldest brother died. Joseph never
forgot it; God's gracious teaching made him feel it was such
an *urgent* thing that men should have the gospel preached to
them, for it was so precious to himself. So to Oxford he
came; there were some very godly men there in the middle
1600s; and Joseph would get up about four o'clock, and
spend about fourteen hours a day in study, missing out one of
his meals to do it. He visited sick people, and also went to
Oxford gaol regularly to preach to the prisoners. But God

Glory be to God, that hath accounted me worthy
to suffer for his Gospell:

Joseph Alleine

ST. MARYS TAUNTON WITH ALLEINE'S MS & SIG.

1620   1660   1700

Charles I | C | OC | Charles II | J | W&M

b.Devizes   ●Oxford Univ.   ●His book
Alarm to the Unconverted
published 1672

J.ALLEINE.1634-68

Preached at Taunton [7YRS] [6YRS] Persecution

had given him a real pastor's heart, and he was not satisfied with less.

About this time he visited one of his father's cousins, who was the minister at Batcombe in Somerset, to tell him how he felt; while he was there he met his lovely daughter Theodosia, and felt he could pray to the Lord to give her to him to be an helpmeet. Six months later the Lord unfolded His good purpose when he was invited to be the assistant minister at Taunton. So to Taunton he came in 1655; he was just 21. Listen to his purpose in preaching to the people there: "I am but the friend of the Bridegroom and my business is but to give you to understand His love and to join your hearts unto Him."

He married his Theodosia, and although they had no children of their own, they started a school, with some boys living in their house, so that there were 20 or 30 in the house, and the day-boys made the school about 50 or 60 in number.

If ever Joseph Alleine heard anyone else at their work before he was, he would be cross with himself, saying, "Oh! how this noise shames me! Does not my master deserve more than theirs?" He studied every morning, then went visiting most afternoons, took the midweek services, and went out in the countryside preaching whenever he could. "Value precious time while time lasts, not when it is lost," he used to say.

But after seven busy, very happy years things in the nation were sad. Those to whom King Charles II gave power were intent on stopping the good Bible preachers; so they made it the rule that every minister had to promise quite a lot of things – and some of them they knew were not in the Bible at all. When Joseph heard what he was being asked to promise, he knew he could not do it – so there was no alternative; he would have to leave. And if these conscientious ministers preached any more, the government would be after them! Now what? Of the 73 ministers in just Somerset alone who couldn't promise, a good number felt they'd better be quiet. Not so Joseph; he knew the Lord had told him to preach, and preach he would – anywhere – until the Lord stopped him. His wife felt just the same about it, although they knew the danger; so they sold their furniture, and were prepared for gaol or banishment, but Joseph went on preaching; house to house, in the villages too, preaching sometimes fourteen times a week, and never had he felt so helped. He prayed for three months' freedom to preach, and the Lord gave him nine; he was arrested for illegal preaching in May 1663; and the magistrates sent him away to Ilchester prison. When he got there the gaoler had gone out; so while he was waiting, he preached from the prison steps, and had gathered 200 to hear him by the time the gaoler returned – and wasn't he angry! He was sent to a room right at the top of the prison, underneath the roof; it was summer, and the roof-tiles got so hot the prisoners took the window panes out to get air – for there were seventy people in that one room already! He was kept in prison over a year, but see how he spent his time; he preached to the other prisoners; when he was later moved to the prison annexe, he was allowed to hold regular services there on Sundays and weekdays, and preached to hundreds; he wrote tracts for the children who lived all round to teach them Bible truths; for his old congregation he wrote out a weekly sermon. "Godliness is heart work, it goes deep and spreads far," he wrote. "Alas that our souls are so narrow, that the waters are so shallow within. How little, how very little, would our love be if He had it all. And have we any of this little to spare for Him? Oh that we might love Him with our little all!"

At last he was released, but the laws were no better. Soon it was ordered that there should be no meetings with more than five people apart from the family. And so many wanted to hear Joseph that he had to divide them up into four parts and teach and preach to them separately. People from the villages all round begged him to go and preach to them as well, in spite of the warrants that were already out again for his arrest; off he went every week. But the prison had affected his health. One day three months after his release, he collapsed after riding sixteen miles out to a congregation, and although he still preached, yet for six whole months he lost the use of his arms, and could not even dress or feed himself, or do any writing. Yet he loved souls so much, he still went on preaching all through the week and twice on Lord's Days. He persuaded a lot of the other good ministers to take the risk of preaching again, and arranged for the secret groups of Christians to be supplied in turn by each little group of preachers. And you know what he was thinking of when Lord Wharton wrote him that letter of encouragement!

The government, which had moved to Oxford because of the Great Plague in London – 10,000 had died in a single week in September 1665 – still plotted the ruin of the Nonconformists; the good ministers were forbidden to come within five miles of where they had been ministers. You can see what that meant to Joseph and Theodosia, taking refuge as they were at Mr. John Mallack's house, a mile outside Taunton; Joseph had enjoyed those walks in the garden there. But what did he do? Why, hold a thanksgiving service the very day before the Five Mile Act was enforced. Then Alleine and his wife moved to Wellington, five miles away, where a dyer offered them shelter at his house 'in a very obscure place', and he was able to carry on preaching there. But the folk going and coming were spotted by their enemies, and the dyer was threatened with prison. What should Joseph do now? Why, go back to Mr. Mallack's house yet again! People wanted to hear him, so he moved from house to house in the town, spending a week or a fortnight at each, teaching and catechizing (question-and-answer) wherever he went. When the authorities suspected a house of a meeting, they ransacked it from top to bottom, but they were worse than burglars, for they took nearly everything away while the poor people watched helplessly – the workman's tools, the merchant's stocks, perhaps even the very bed. But *still* the meetings went on.

One day they were in Mr. John Mallack's house 'Fullands' holding a thanksgiving service; Joseph was going to Devizes to try to get better at the mineral waters there. But what is this? Officers of the law interrupted, and the meeting, at which 120 people were gathered, was broken up, and Joseph is to spend another three months in Ilchester gaol. The morning he was released, he encouraged his fellow-prisoners to remember their prison comforts with thankfulness to God and to go home praising Him; to depend more on God who had thus taken such care of them while they had been there although they could hardly have expected it; and to love Him and one another more. "Let divine mercy be as oil to the flame of your love," he said.

But he was so ill; though he preached eighteen more months, he had to give up finally, losing all use of his limbs, his wife nursing him lovingly night and day. "Who in all the earth should admire and commend this love if I should not?" he said while lying there helpless and paralysed. He was taken to Bath for the benefit of the waters there; ill as he was, he preached the gospel to the society there; on the way back to the house, he would ask those who carried him to take him to the schools where he spoke to the children, or to visit the poor and widows of the town. On Sundays he and his wife had 60 or 70 children at his lodging to teach them.

But his life was done; a full life brought to a close, and on 17th November 1668 a crowd of hundreds disobeyed the laws

to follow his body to the grave in his old church in Taunton. He was 34! His dear folk never forgot him; and even today there are churches that claim to have been formed by him. And so he *reached* the mark set before him, the prize of the high calling of God in Christ Jesus.

One of the congregations to which Joseph Alleine ministered in those days of persecution was at Newhouse and Luppitt, near Honiton. Baptists had formed a church there in 1652, and when in the 1660s their meetings were forbidden, they continued just the same. There were still added to them 'such as should be saved,' and baptisms were administered by night in the open-air pool fed from a spring in the woods. Newhouse is 900 feet above the sea, and in those days it was on the border of three counties, so that if the authorities approached they could escape over the county border beyond reach.

There stood the early meeting-house next to a little cottage with a connecting doorway. By the doorway was a window through which preachers standing in the cottage could preach to those in the meeting-house, and if need be give warning of an enemy's approach so that they could escape to the nearby woods.

Joseph Alleine was actually on his way to preach at Luppitt when he was arrested and taken to Ilchester gaol. In the gaol, as soon as he could, he sat down and wrote a letter to them on 11th October 1665. This is what he wrote:

"Dearly beloved christians, You were the people that were last upon my heart before my taking up (i.e. his arrest), and had I not been made a prisoner I think I had in a few hours after the time of my apprehension been with you...I bless the Lord to hear His work doth not cease among you.

Know, dear christians, that the bonds of the gospel are not tedious through grace unto us; that Christ is a Master worth suffering for; that there is really enough in religion to defray all our charges; that you may build upon it that you can never be losers by Jesus Christ; that Christ's prison is better than the world's paradise; that the Divine attributes are alone an all-sufficient livelihood: that the influences of Heaven and shines of God's Countenance are sufficient to lighten the darkest dungeon, and to perfume and sweeten the nauseous prison to a poor believer; that if you can bring faith and patience and the assurance of Divine favour with you to a prison, you will live comfortably in spite of earth and hell...These are truths that the prisoners of Christ can in a measure seal unto; and I would have you to be more soundly assured of, and established on...Come on, beloved Christians, come on; slack not your pace but give diligence to the full assurance of hope unto the end, and be ye followers of them, who, through faith and patience, now inherit the promises... Will any of you think of returning into Egypt? God forbid: a little patience and Christ will come... He is not a Christian indeed, that cannot be content to tarry for his preferment in another world: cast upon it, my brethren, that your kingdom is not of this world; that here you must have tribulations, and that all is well as long as we are secured for eternity....

Farewell, dear brethren; farewell in the Lord,
I am, Your in the bonds of the Lord Jesus,

Joseph Alleine.

In the houses where he used to stay for a little while, he carefully and lovingly observed everyone's ways; and when the time came for him to leave, he would call them one by one into his room, and people noticed that when each came out, hardly anyone had dry eyes after such a loving personal talk.

In his Taunton days he used to spend five afternoons from about half-past one to seven o'clock, visiting three or four families each afternoon: he would tell each family the day before that he was coming, hoping they would allow him to begin with prayer and then speak with them about their souls, the older ones singly and the young ones together. When he had visited all the families in the town in turn, he would start all over again. He would try to get them to promise, each night before they went to bed, to ask themselves how their *souls* had prospered, so praying to God more thoughtfully for His grace.

When he was lying paralysed, a friend asked him how he could be so contented. "What!" he said, "is God my Father, Jesus Christ my Saviour, and the Spirit my sweet friend, and heaven my inheritance, and shall I not be content without limbs and health? Through grace I am fully satisfied with my Father's pleasure...I have lived a sweet life by the promises, and I hope through grace, can die by a promise; it is the promises of God which are everlasting, that will stand by us: nothing but God in them will serve us in a day of affliction." Often he would say as he woke in the morning, "Now we have one day more; here is one more for God; now let us live well this day; work hard for souls; lay up much treasure in heaven this day, for we have but a few to live."

"But what can this child say to us?"

EARLY in 1601 little Herbert Palmer was born at Wingham, six miles from Canterbury. He had a good father and mother who, beside being a knight and lady, were God-fearing people; and as soon as her little baby boy could listen to a story, the mother told him about the people of the Bible so simply and lovingly that when he was only four or five, he would run to his mother and say, "Can I listen to something about God?" And it seems as though there was something good in his heart toward the God of Israel, because these feelings did not wear off, as they often do in children, but kept on growing. When he was asked what he wanted to do when he grew up, he said, "To be a minister of Jesus Christ." "Oh," said his friends to test him, "you could do better than that; ministers are often despised and hated." "Never mind that," he would say, "If the world hates me, God will love me." So it was God Himself who gave him that desire to learn of Him. Once, when he was only five, he was found crying over the story of Joseph, which he had read in his Bible; and there he would sit learning the chapters off by heart!

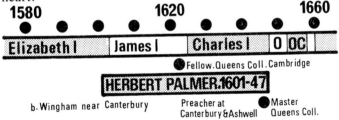

Herbert: Palmer-Vicar.

HERBERT PALMER

I wonder if you like learning French? Herbert was taught
the language so young that he never remembered learning it,
but could speak it as well as English. I expect you might say,
What good did that do? But God has His way to make use of
such things, as you will see presently. So that although he
never went to France in his life, yet if any visitor came over,
he would ask questions about that land, and listen for hours,

so that he learnt all about the way God was working in that land, although so many godly people were hunted out of it, a lot of them settling in his own native Kent.

When he was old enough, off he went to school and afterward to college; you would find him at his books after everyone else had gone off to their sport; he would say, "The best pastime is when time is best passed." So at Queens College, Cambridge he became M.A., and when he was 22 he was made a Fellow; which meant that he could take paying pupils. Well, he had enough from home to be quite comfortable, so that he did not need to teach; but he would not take a Fellow's place just for the sake of the name, so he was glad to take many students and teach them truly. He would have them in his room, and teach them and pray with them, and watch over them and seek to lead them to the Lord. And after he had been doing this for just a year, he was appointed a minister of Jesus Christ. *A change for the better* he had longed for.

Visiting his home near Canterbury, some of his friends invited him to preach in the Cathedral there, and the Lord helped him greatly, so that many folk spoke to others about it. Now Mr. Delme was the good minister of the French church in Canterbury at that time, and he heard about it. He thought to himself, 'I am sure it would do my people good to hear him; I will go to see him myself and give him an invitation.' So off he went to Wingham, and when they met and got talking, a friendship sprang up like that between David and Jonathan, that only death could interrupt. And Mr. Delme went home very pleased with himself, for he was able to arrange for his new friend to preach another sermon, this time at St. George's Church in the city there. And the more people heard Mr. Palmer preach, the more they wanted to hear. At length they invited him to come to Canterbury for good; and when he agreed, arrangements were soon completed for him to preach every week in Alphage church. No-one was more pleased than Mr. Delme to have such a friend for a neighbour. So he came to preach every so often at the French church too – you will remember his French? When he came into the pulpit there for the first

ASHWELL CHURCH

time, he looked so small! An old French gentlewoman said out loud, "Alas, but what can this child say to us?" And those sitting nearby felt the same. But *when* they had listened all through, the old lady spoke for them all, and lifting up her hands to heaven, blessed God for what she had heard! It teaches us not to make up our minds before we have listened for ourselves!

But after a number of years, Mr. Palmer was called away from his friends at Canterbury, to become the vicar of Ashwell, Hertfordshire; he was 32 now. Every Lord's Day he preached twice, and tried hard to use plain words so that the very simplest person could understand what he meant. He often matched the Word of God with the Providence of God at that moment, so that the two went together, and spoke with one voice. Before the sermon on a Lord's Day afternoon, he would ask everyone to send their children to learn by question-and-answer method; and so many came, he had to carry on at home afterwards, and have someone to help him with them too!

When anyone could read, he was anxious to give them a Bible; and if they had no opportunity to learn to read, as soon as they had really learnt the scripture doctrines well, he would give them five shillings to encourage them. And as time went by, the children grew up, and had children of their own, their homes reflected what they had been taught. And he got the village people to promise to come to worship instead of spending their time asleep or playing, fighting or stealing.

At home, his aim was, a garden without weeds! Twice daily he prayed with his household, not allowing anyone to be away; and read to them out of the Bible at the same time. As he was not married, he had servants and maids; and for his family he had young men from the noble families around to stay there, and had a schoolmaster for them, all at home.

When the sabbath was coming, he wanted to get ready beforehand, the food prepared and so on; and if he found that anyone had not been able to get out to worship because of the cooking, he would not eat any of that course.

When he read his Bible himself, as well as explaining it in the family, he would write down notes of what he felt was taught; and last thing before he went to bed, he would write his diary of what had happened that day, the successes and disappointments, the mercies and the crosses, and the failings he had observed in himself; and by degrees he got to know himself better. The old writer who tells his story says, he walked with God more evenly, and his sun shone more

constantly; although the sun's constant brightness produces less admiration than some blazing star that appears but for a little while, because men usually more admire things rare than excellent.

Next he was called to help the Westminster Assembly, and so he came to London; and preaching where he was asked, sometimes found himself preaching for six or eight hours on a Lord's Day. His friends tried to persuade him to go easier – it was more than his weak body could stand, they said. He replied that his strength would go anyway, even if he did nothing; so he could not spend it better than in God's service. It was a rule with him never to decline ministering the word of God whenever he was asked, whether in private or public, if he were possibly able to do so.

Finally, he was made in 1644 Master of Queens College, Cambridge, where he had gone all those years before. He tried to think of everything; books for the Library, help to support numerous scholars otherwise too poor to go, who taught them – he called the college his Great Care. When he was giving away to those in need, he did his very utmost to make sure they did not know where the help had come from.

But his time was done. Someone visited him in his weakness, hoping he would get better; so they read Isaiah 38. And then he himself prayed. It is a very solemn thing to listen to a dying man's prayer; he had had a better night, and this is how he prayed:

"Blessed be God that hath been so good to us this night.

Great God, heal the sinfulness of my nature. Pardon all my transgressions. Take from me a heart of unbelief, that I may not depart from Thee, the living God. Deliver me from temptation. Accept of Jesus Christ for me. Teach me to improve all providences, to live upon the promises. Let Christ be my life. O Lord, let me never shrink from Thee.

Lord, turn the hearts of this nation, and all our hearts. Turn the heart of the king. Sanctify the Parliament and make them faithful. Bless the Assembly, and make them faithful, and upright with Thee. Let not the army do unworthily, but what Thou wouldst have them to do. Bless all the ministers.

Lord, do good to Scotland, and to the churches in France. Bless New England, and foreign plantations.

Lord, provide a faithful man for Queens College; a faithful man for this place (New Church, Westminster); a faithful pastor for those in the country.

Lord, remember all those that have showed kindness to me, and have taken pains with me, and recompense them. Thou hast promised that he which giveth a cup of water in the name of a disciple, and he that receiveth a prophet in the name of a prophet, shall have a prophet's reward."

They brought him a tiny bit of something to eat, and he forgot to ask a blessing on it. Realising this, straightway he prayed:

"Lord, pardon my neglect and forgetfulness of Thee; and deliver me from temptation, and the evil of temptation. Thou art holy if Thou shouldest forsake us; our fathers trusted in Thee and were delivered. Lord, glorified be Thy name in my poor spirit, and let none of Thy people ever see me shrink from Thee, for Jesus Christ's sake."

So the good man departed for a better country, that is, an heavenly; he was 46. Lovingly they buried his body in the New Church, Westminster, where he had so often preached.

Another minister in this part of the country was Dr. Staunton: he was once suspended for a time from preaching for refusing to read *The Book of Sports* from his pulpit. He was later one of the divines at the Westminster Assembly. After he retired he spent his time giving out catechisms and copies of Baxter's *Call* to the poorer families in the neighbourhood.

He told once of how he was going to Hempstead to preach; and as he went along on the road near Langley he was thinking and meditating on the wonderful gospel he had to preach: to think of the love of God calling such a one as he was when thousands more noble, wise and learned went on in willing ignorance! he could not help the tears coming to his eyes, and his heart was filled with abundant joy at the Lord's mercy.

He knew the Bible so well people used to say his head would do instead of a concordance! Sitting down to write his letters, he would add as a PS at the end three or four scripture verses: sometimes it may be they meant more to the reader than the letter itself.

It was the same when he was visiting, or met a friend in the street: when they came to say goodbye, he would say, 'Now let me leave one scripture text with you, and then you can think of it when I have gone.' Alone or with others, when he prayed he would kneel on the ground, even in a crowd, and he would say, 'The humblest gesture as well as the humblest spirit fits us when we pray."

So we must come to the end of the book. But may we go on learning the lessons they have showed us, and may we know that *change for the better*, a new birth as it says in John 3, to live like they did, for the honour and glory of Jesus Christ. To live like that is to live a life that will never end.